Holding Hands…

The four principles of raising children…And how to heal society in the process

Bernadette Mather

Copyright © 2016 by Bernadette Mather

First Printing: 2016.

ISBN-13: 978-1537257266

To Etta-Lucy and Adam.
You inspire me, and fill me with joy every day.

PREFACE

After moving from the North East to the great City of London, and following a career that took me to some wonderful places in the world, I woke up one day preparing myself for the greatest adventure of my life – being a parent.

In anticipation of giving birth, I searched the shelves for books about raising children, and bought a few. The advice was all very 'solid': what to feed them; what time to put them to bed; the pros and cons of nursery; going back to work; how to discipline them; how to introduce the naughty step. There seemed to be endless sources of advice. When the baby arrived, I was careful to follow the advice; remembering to watch the clock to make sure she didn't oversleep in the afternoon (otherwise, according to the 'guru', she wouldn't sleep at night); making sure I planned the afternoon stroll at the correct time, so as not to change the routine; carefully selecting educational toys to optimise her learning ability; making sure I always remembered to book the baby yoga class, and of course, worrying that I hadn't always been able to find organic carrots in the supermarket, but was feeding my daughter the same type of carrots that I had been raised on for thirty years (shock, horror).

With all of this newly acquired knowledge crammed into

my head, I almost felt that I had stopped listening to my own instincts as a mother and a person. Some of the advice worked, and some of it didn't. As each day passed, I learned new things such as not all babies sleep for a certain number of hours but, just like adults, some need more and some need less. While all the books I read helped, I just felt that there was something missing in the 'how to' childcare section. It wasn't until my second child arrived that I discovered what was missing. I had dumbed down my intuition, my natural parenting skills, because I hadn't formulated them or packaged them in my head the way the gurus had. All the learning was good but pieces were missing. So, I gave myself a good talking to and tuned in to my parental instincts and what I packaged in my head; creating from that four guiding principles I then used, and still use, each day for raising my children. I found that following the four principles made parenting easier, more enjoyable, and more rewarding. Everything just seems to flow better. An added bonus was that I was much happier myself.

It was during this 'tuning into' my instincts that I came across a story in a newspaper about a remarkable lady, Fatemah Golmakani; whose teenage son, Milad, was stabbed and killed that made me realise that my role as a parent had far wider reaching consequences than making sure that my children were well behaved, worked hard at school, and got a good job. Read her story in the first part of my book. It made me realise that my job as a parent had an effect on society, that raising children well is laying the foundations of our society. If we get the foundations right by creating children who love themselves and respect others, the dream of a society without crime would not be far away as good children become good adults, who create a good society. I thank Fatemah for inspiring me to put pen to paper.

As I raised my children, I realised that these four principles on which all of my parenting was based made up many aspects of parenting we often struggle with, such as discipline, confidence-building, and attitude. Once I realised what impact these four principles had, I wanted to share my message in the hope that our children would grow up happy in a happy society without conflict. I truly believe that this is possible and that these principles, if we all follow them, are powerful enough to rid the world of hatred and wars (imagine that as a side effect of good parenting) and that our children will have happy fulfilled lives. I have 'packaged' these foundations to share with you and hope that your children and you will benefit from following them. I thank you for taking your precious time because you care about that very precious gift you have been given... your child.

FOREWORD

Your parenting today affects how your adult child turns out, and how our society will look tomorrow. Your influence over another person has never had so much impact. You are shaping the future as the clock ticks. This really is the most important job you will ever do in your life.

Do you want to create a happy, confident adult?

Do you want to create someone with good values, who will never be tempted to steal or hurt people?

Do you want to dramatically reduce the risk of your child ever taking drugs or too much alcohol?

Do you want to be a major force in creating a more crime free, caring society?

Your starting point is to recognise that anyone can give birth, but not everyone can become a true parent, a good parent. Every day YOU are standing in the shoes of a creator. You are responsible for guiding your son or daughter towards becoming an amazing adult.

This guide covers the four principles that are essential for a healthy, loving child. If you live by this guide, I guarantee that your healthy, happy children will turn into happy, responsible adults. I guarantee that you will contribute to the welfare of your society because children who are loved grow into adults who are loved, and adults who are loved generally want to love others, so eventually as parents, we really can help stop wars and create paradise on earth.

"Mothers and fathers provide the greatest influence over their children. Therefore, anyone who becomes a parent plays an important part in creating members of their society. Ultimately, our parents bear responsibility for how people behave towards others in society."

Turn the pages to discover the perfect formula for raising your child. In a world where we are inundated with books about raising children, this guide provides a simple formula that underpins and eases the pressures and, dare I say, the pain of raising happy, successful children.

You will discover that you can be more than just an average parent; you can be an excellent parent. By understanding and consistently following four key principals, you will discover the joys of bringing up happy children.

Most parenting guides ask for your head when you read. I ask for your head, BUT I also ask for your heart and your intuition. This really is the magic formula for raising children. I call it magic because the four rules make other things happen as if by magic. Imagine not having to remind your children to tidy their rooms… they offer to do it… really it can happen.

This guide provides advice on both the emotional and practical issues of raising children; many of the big issues, such as the first day at school, and some of the issues that feel big at the time, such as little Tommy refusing to eat his carrots.

The four rules, and yes, they are rules, provide a platform for your child's happiness, self–esteem, behaviour, social citizenship, and their own future relationships.

When you finish reading this guide, you will have the knowledge to:

- Build a successful relationship with the most important person in your life, your child
-Deal with behavioural issues
- Talk to your child
- Set limits
- Help reduce the chances of your child having mental health issues
- Reduce the chances of your child becoming addicted to drugs or alcohol. *
- Contribute to a better society

Every aspect of childhood can be treated with this magic formula. It really does work.

The reward for you? From this day forward, your life will be peppered with examples of how much your child loves you – believe me, you will never experience a more satisfying emotion. Yes, parenting is a full time job, but it is the highest paid job, as the payment is love in its purest form.

*Of course, some people become addicts not because they haven't had good parents but because, according to research, they carry the addiction gene. However, there is evidence that genetic addiction can be managed more easily if the person has a greater sense of self-worth and self-confidence.

Why this formula works in EVERY country in the world

When we travel to different countries, watch the news, see documentaries on TV, we see cultural differences in the way we raise our children. Asia has a reputation for placing high importance on education, and we often hear about 'Tiger Mums' putting pressure on their little darlings to achieve. In Italy and Spain, children of all ages are found in restaurants at all times of the day and night, whereas this is a rarer sight in England. Different countries and cultures have different ways. These four rules work across all boundaries, they are universal in their ability to improve a child's wellbeing and happiness.

Whatever the culture, circumstances of life, or education structure, this formula works to create a confident, self-assured person who will have the best life they can in their surroundings. Life for some people is tough, circumstances can be grim, but without parents who follow these simple four rules, it would be far worse. For others who live in a more privileged society, life can be good and with parents who follow these rules life gets a whole lot better. Whatever your country, culture, beliefs, or social circumstances, you owe your child the honour of following these rules.

By following this guide, you will have a child with self-worth, love, and self-confidence; a child with these attributes will most often wish to spread love and confidence to others… it's just the way it works. Make sure your child gets the best chance of happiness, no matter what your social, political, or financial situation.

1

No going back!

You are a new parent; you have just brought a new life into the world. Bombarded with advice from friends and relatives; grabbing those 'perfect parenting' books by the side of your bed when you have a moment; you are bemused, confused, and a little scared. There are only two things that are true at this stage.

ONE
It is normal to feel like this.

TWO
You have the potential to be not just a good but a brilliant parent.

You have the ability to be the perfect parent, we all do. By following this guide you will create a well behaved, happy, confident child. Moreover, in eighteen years' time, you will have created a happy, loving adult, who will carry your legacy of good parenting through generations of your family. How amazing is that!

Now happiness and love may sound like 'soft' attributes, but did you know that people who don't have this in their lives are statistically more likely to suffer physically? Not many people are aware that their positive actions and attitude can protect and improve their child's health. A major research programme carried out in October 2011, by neuroscientist Vincent J Felitti, on Adverse Childhood Experiences revealed that traumatic life experiences, often buried or denied, and surprisingly common, had a profound effect on health, addiction, and death. He said, 'Many adult health problems and chronic diseases are determined decades earlier, in childhood – not by diseases of childhood as once was thought to be the case, but by life experiences'.

You can help limit the chances of your child becoming depressed, having eating disorders, becoming dependent on drugs and alcohol, or becoming a shopping addict*. No, the shopping issue isn't frivolous. This is a real addiction, affecting many people, and has far reaching consequences, such as the debt it brings to families which can destroy family life.

With good parenting, you create a positive and loving child and adult. By following this guide, you are virtually guaranteed, yes guaranteed, a well-balanced, happy, loving member of your family.

Now, don't be fooled as you get comfortable on the sofa, it is not always easy; dare I say, it is sometimes boring, BUT it is THE most rewarding job you will EVER find. In this guide, I have mentioned a few stories that highlight the reward I have received from parenting. I hope you enjoy reading them as much as I enjoyed experiencing them. When you find yourself in your story, write it down and keep it in a safe place. Look at it from time to time and feel the warm glow you get inside.

That glow will NEVER fade. (In fact, go on jump to page x and read one little story now…) but come back to this page and start to create a happy life for the most precious gift you have, your child.?"

"Parents are powerful beyond what they know their power to be."

You may not realise it but you are on the brink of creating a major change to your society, to humanity. By raising a happy child, you are now a key person in altering the 'health' of your society and future generations within that society. Did you even realise just how powerful you are? Quick, just get up now and walk over to the mirror. Look at yourself. Whatever your persona, you're about to add another dimension to the person you see in the mirror. You are a major force now in improving your society. You can help to create a society where there is respect for others; respect for others' property; admiration for those who help others; understanding of education for the advancement of the human race and spirit; appreciation of creative talent; a willingness to contribute to the financial stability of the community, nationally and internationally; empathy, and a willingness to help those less fortunate.

Here are four good reasons to be a good parent:

1 – You feel emotionally rewarded
2 – Your child is positive, loving to others, and mentally healthy
3 – You leave a parenting legacy to your children
4 – You help to create a 'paradise society'

What I am referring to with a 'paradise society' is that how you raise this one child is another step in reducing day to day crimes that happen on your street, on your friend's and family's streets. Generation after generation of good parenting will change this dramatically. People who feel angry with their lot, and rejected by friends and family commit crimes. Criminals have not had 'good' parenting; they are angry and sad. People can do BAD things when they are fundamentally SAD about something or someone. There are very few people who are 'bad', but many who do bad things because they lack love and guidance in their life. Gang culture is particularly attractive to those who don't feel loved or wanted in their family. When people join gangs, they feel like part of a 'family'. We are human; we need to 'belong', to feel important to someone. The words from the musical, West Side Story, 'no one is an orphan when they are in a gang' rings true. They do not feel loved by their own family so they reach out to a group of so-called 'friends'. Their confidence and self-esteem is low. The other gang members make them feel like they belong and that someone cares, that they have a part to play in the world (albeit a dangerous one). To maintain that sense of belonging, they do things to conform to the gangs' requirements, and join in the revenge and knife culture. You only have to read the newspaper to find out what the results are.

People involved in the criminal world will generally tell you that they never had a parent or an adult who told them they were an amazing person.

"Have you ever met a happy bully?
Someone who feels loved and has a
sense of self-worth and does not bully
others?"

Sad = Bad

Bad = Sad

"Giving love creates love. If your child
is loved, she won't want to pass on her
sadness to someone else by bullying
them."

For some unlucky children, often their sense of self-worth is only attained by joining a gang. The gang makes him feel like someone, like he belongs, like he is useful.

Now before all of you who are reading this think, 'oh, that's not in my world, my little Tommy won't join a gang, as we don't live near a council estate', think again. Little Tommy may not join a gang on the streets, but what about the gang taking cocaine when he gets to university. Will he join in to feel as though he 'belongs'? This is little Tommy's gang. Not on the streets, but in the chic night clubs in town. Not with people who don't have money, but people who have the cash and don't know how to spend it wisely.

Look at how many middle class teenage girls start drinking alcohol. Girls who start drinking at an early age do it to join in with the crowd (the gang) or because it makes them forget about feeling sad. It's not about the social class your children are in or where they live; it's about feeling important, loved, and wanted. It's what we ALL need and if we don't FEEL it, we look to find it somehow with someone, and sometimes it's with people who are doing good things and sometimes it's with people who are doing bad things.

Then there are those who do the complete opposite. They may withdraw from others to hide, or they may fight against others to cover up their true feelings of lack of self-worth. Those children may retreat to their bedrooms, play too many video games, or eat too much junk food to somehow lessen their feelings of low self-worth.

A sense of self-worth is essential to the human condition. We do better in everything we try when we appreciate ourselves. Without it, our basic human requirement is stifled. If you learn nothing else from this guide, know that to assist your child to have self-worth you have passed on an incredible gift. No matter where you come from or where you live, everyone needs a sense of self-worth to have a chance to live a life free from depression, addiction, and anti-social activity.

I was very moved when I read a newspaper story of Fatemah Golmakani; whose teenage son, Milad, was stabbed and killed by a gang one night on his way home. Four men were responsible and they are now serving prison sentences. The mother of the boy insisted on being in contact with the killers and has sold her family jewellery in order to facilitate her visits to see them in prison. She says that she wants to look after them as clearly no one cared for them; she wants to give them a feeling of self-worth, because she knows that they would not have committed such an offence had they had self-respect and love. She understands this. Even a mother who has had her child taken away from this life, and could choose to be bitter and hate the murderers, can see that the sadness and low self-esteem the killers had were the underlying causes of her son's death. She wanted to be their parent, she felt sad that they had not had the love, and therefore respect, for other people that her own son had. What an incredible lady.

It really is that simple. If we don't experience love, our self-esteem will be low, and we will find it difficult to have loving relationships. Those that are not able to have loving relationships have a lack of self-respect and respect for others. If you don't respect people, it is so much easier to commit anti-social acts. Everyone who has a child has the chance to show that child love and self-respect, and in turn, improve our society.

Lack of love = lack of self-esteem = lack of ability to form loving relationships = no desire to be a positive force in society = reacting against or withdrawing from society.

The reason why bullies are bullies at school, the reason people steal, the reason people take drugs, the reason why people abuse their children is simply because they were not loved and raised appropriately when they were children. But wait, I am not saying that everyone who was not loved as a child will grow up to be anti-social. Many people who are parents now were raised in very harsh circumstances where smacking was the norm. It is certainly not a natural progression for these children to become unruly adults, but some of them will. People are far less likely to want to hurt others if they come from families where love and respect are the norm.

There is the question of the pattern of parenting from generation to generation which goes two ways. People either copy their own upbringing or they react against it and do the opposite (generally if it was viewed in a negative way). It is good, as a parent, to analyse your own childhood and how it affected you. When you reflect, think about how your parents built you as part of society's foundation, and how you are now a positive contributor (you must be to be reading this. You care.)

Just for a moment, let's look at our current choices for improving aspects of society. We can:

1. Listen to politicians debating legalising/non-legalising drugs. (No resolve. Cost of debate)?

2. Buy more burglar alarms. Build more private gated residencies. (More personal cost)?

3. Fund more psychologists to work out why more teenagers are suffering from depression (Cost to society)?

4. Fund more eating disorder specialists to help those in that cycle of self-abuse (Cost to society)?

5. Teach people how to be great parents who will raise secure, happy children who contribute to our society. (Free! And it works!)?

Numbers one to four are what billions of pounds are spent on year after year. If we do number 5 correctly, the outcome would mean happier people, as well as having a positive financial aspect to it, that of saving millions of pounds on drugs, eating disorders, and alcohol related illnesses.

Let's follow the example of the mother who sold her jewellery to help the young people who murdered her son. She knows how our society can change through good parenting. She knows that we need to make sure our children know they are valued, loved, useful, and important to their family and our society. She has lost a son, but she recognises the key reasons why people commit acts of great unkindness in our society. So, what are we going to do about it? What are you going to do about it? You, as a parent, have a massive impact on the future of your society.

You can change the world, and you can experience raising amazing children who love themselves, you, their community, and their world (as well as eat their carrots, don't have tantrums in the supermarket and don't become grumpy, unsociable teenagers).

So what can we do now, today?

How do we raise our children and turn them into caring contributors to our society? There is no lack of baby books that provide good advice on a child's routine, how to discipline a child, what food to eat, and how often. When making my own decisions to help me to be a good mother, I imagined myself as an alien from another planet in the universe having to learn about raising a child. I discovered there were all sorts of books; from how to establish a routine after 11 weeks, through to potty training, dealing with tantrums, and looking after your sensitive child etc.

It was so complicated, and there was so much to learn, but overall I found that there were simply four very clear, simple principles leaping off the pages. Over and over again, these words jumped out of the pages, hundreds and hundreds of pages saying the same thing over and over again. It became very clear to me that if these four areas were addressed, some of the more practical issues, such as stopping the tantrum in the supermarket, could be addressed with ease – yes, with ease! It became clear to me (as it will to you) that there are only four principles to raising children, and if you stick to these rules throughout your children's lives; boy, are you powerful. You will have amazing children, who will in turn become amazing adults.

Now, I have promised to share the four principles of raising children, but there is a catch. These four rules will only work if you establish your relationship with your child.

To have a relationship – the meaning is, **'To have a connection by the fact of being related or associated with a person'.**

The connection you have with your child will dictate their behaviour from this day on. I would like you, from this moment on, to think of this relationship as being as essential as food. You need to provide the right food (relationship) throughout the child's life to nurture your child into a great adult. The next time you feed those mushed up carrots to your child, think about your relationship. How have you developed your relationship with your child today?

This isn't new. While many parenting experts disagree on various aspects, the one thing that they agree upon is that a relationship is critical. It is the foundation for discipline, contentment, and provides a platform for academic education to flourish.

So how do you create a connection, a relationship? How long have you known this person? A week? A month? A year? Three years? What is your connection at this moment in time?

Many of you will say 'of course I have a relationship, after all I am the parent'. Well… yes you are, but while you may feel that strong connection right now, how will you hold onto it? How will it be maintained for the next 18 years (and beyond)? How will it change throughout the years? Your child is six months old now and what is your relationship? Protector, provider, comforter? Your child is thirteen now, what is your relationship? Protector, provider, comforter, taxi service, education support, relationship adviser? You see, we change according to our children's requirements. Our relationship changes from year to year. Keep an eye on the relationship. Understand your child's needs.

Summary of your role as they grow

Age 0 – 3 you are the protector, provider, someone who comforts

Age 4 – 6 you are the protector, provider, someone who listens, the expert

Age 7 – 10 you are the guide, the person who knows all the answers, the comforter

Age 11 – 14 you are the guide, the comforter, the taxi service, the fixer, the expert

Age 15 – 18 you are the listener, the re-assurer, the hot

chocolate maker (when they are studying for their exams), skills coach (making sure they will be able to cook for themselves, and change a light bulb when they are adults).

Age 21+ you are there when they need you, but your role as guide has been usurped by friends and famous people.

As you read on, think about your relationship, how it is now, and how it will change. Above all, keep the connection as it underpins everything that follows.

So you've made it to this page, thank you, and now allow me to share the magic formula with you. The formula has four principles. They are:

LOVE

HUG

PLAY

GUIDE

This formula is what you must adhere to from now until well... forever.

Sounds easy - but don't be fooled. These four rules require your time, your energy, your commitment, and your heart. It is no easy journey, but it works. And when you walk down the street with your five, ten, fifteen, twenty-five, forty-five year old who makes you proud, is happy, and brings joy to other people's lives every day, you will be very happy that you have focused on these principles. That is a promise!

2

RULE ONE: LOVE

So, what is the process of loving, and how does it start?

How do we start to love someone? We start to love someone by creating an attachment. All humans and animals need an attachment in order to love. So mothers have a natural attachment when carrying their child. Mothers must continue this attachment (not easy for all mothers). Fathers must start the attachment from day one, through feeding and cuddling their baby.

According to James Prescott, Disney, following a study into the root causes of violence, said that as we are nurtured and influenced by the physical and the emotional connection to our mother and father, our conscience is set. So, in this way, you can see how your treatment of your child has a much greater and wider influence. How you create your attachment with your child influences the development of their conscience, and therefore, how they view society and their role in it. Psychologists often theorise about what creates conscience. I wonder how many violent prisoners had a great attachment with their parents. How were their consciences formed? Many of them were 'shaped' with a lack of emotional connection, and it has had an impact on the rest of their lives.

Another source backs up the huge influence that parental connection has on our upbringing. The authors of 'A General Theory of Life' explain that mammals who grow up in the absence of the influence of limbic regulation are "jagged and incomplete". He tells us that, "central to this incompleteness is the missing foundation for the development of the entire suite of peacemaker capacities – including the basis of what we would call 'conscience'." In other words, without the parental connection, it is almost impossible to be a considerate member of a society.

Another expert, Bruce Perry, links bonding, attachment, and conscience to this simple evaluation.

People = Pleasure

When bonding and attachment unfold as nature intends, the connection between a mother and her baby remains unbroken after birth. A mother will reliably tend to her baby's cries and coos in an engaged, responsive way, and delights in his delight, and he comes to associate her with all that is good. Mama = Pleasure. This association lays the foundation for the child over the course of the first three years, when the brain is developing rapidly, to internalize a myriad of complex associations as a foundation for a healthy self ("I'm effective in the world", "I can trust others to be there for me" "I make people happy", etc.) and also for his brain to eventually hardwire the broader association. People = Pleasure. It is this People = Pleasure association that underlies civilized behaviour.

Therefore, we have the first act of love – ATTACHMENT.

So, the foundations are set with our attachment and the child's conscience is developing. Like your child's body, when the seed of love is sown, it is small and needs nourishment. Your child needs nourishment through seeing and feeling your love, which is vital to his/her development.

So let's look at showing and feeling love.

We all say we love. We love our parents, our partners, our children, our friends, but how do we express this, and how does the person we love know that we love them? I find it very sad when people lose their parents and they say, 'I never knew just how much she/he loved me because he/she never said it'. We are all human; we can't read others' thoughts. We have to make our love obvious. We often don't because we are scared; scared of looking silly, scared of losing who we are (strong, emotionally stable, not soft), scared of opening our hearts because we may get hurt and we may not be loved in return. Well, if you don't express your love, the person you love will never know. If you do express your love, there is a chance it may be returned, a BIG chance.

At this point, I am going to divert a little because I want to reinforce to you just how easy it is to love children... by contrasting how difficult and complicated it can be to love as adults.

As adults, we give and we require different signs of love. We become more emotionally complex as we grow, due to our differing life experiences. Did you know that there are five core signs that adults require recognised by 'love experts'. Our love 'needs' fit into five categories. They are:
- Giving gifts
- Words of affirmation (telling someone how well they have done, how good they look, how clever they are)
- Spending time
- Acts of service
- Touch

Gary Chapman talks about the 'Five Love Languages'. The theory is that we all have signs of language we respond to. There are five, and each person will show a preference for one over the others.

The five love languages are:

Words of affirmation –
Telling your partner how good they look, how lovely dinner was etc. (People who need this one more than others tend to be those who lacked such words of affirmation from their parents).

Time –

Many people simply value people spending time with them. This doesn't just mean being in the same physical space, but also giving them your attention. That is to say, you can be sitting in the same room but if you are reading the newspaper, you are not giving your time to them.

Acts of Service –

Many people respond to receiving help and assistance. Doing the gardening or vacuuming, cleaning their car, painting the bedroom. Of course, the person delivering these acts must go about their tasks with good grace, otherwise it is not an act of love but an act of duty.

Gifts -

Since the beginning of the human race we have given each other gifts. We shouldn't confuse spending lots of money with giving a gift. Often a low cost gift can mean much more than a very expensive gift. To forget a gift on a special day, birthdays, anniversaries, or Christmas is very upsetting for someone who values gift giving and as it is built into our culture this means most of us!

Touch –

We all vary in terms of how much touch we require from our partner. Everyone requires some, no matter how little. It is a very basic human need.

Get that pen and paper out again NOW and think about this for a while. What do you need from your partner? What do they need from you? If you have a strong connection now with your partner, I guarantee it is because your 'love needs' are being met by them, and theirs by you. Most relationship break ups happen because the other person's needs are either not understood or met.

Let me explain further. Take, for example, person A. This person likes their partner to spend time with them. They don't value gifts (although they may not dislike receiving them!) and they require a lot of physical touch from their partner. Person B responds to words of affirmation and acts of service.

An ideal night out for person A is for them both to spend

time together whilst getting ready, being present together at an event with lots of body contact and always holding hands. Person B, will enjoy being told how attractive they look, and how smart they are and will appreciate their shirt or dress having been ironed for them.

If person B was rushing back from work, didn't spent much time with the partner getting ready and was physically distant when they went out, person A would not be happy. Correspondingly, if person A hadn't ironed the dress/shirt, knowing person B would be rushing and didn't mention how they looked, then person B would be unhappy.

So, that's how complex it is to love as adults. Now back to children and the good news….

The good news is that when it comes to young children it really is simple. Children need universal signs of love that all children need. It is NOT complicated at all.

- Children need to be cared for (food, hygiene, warmth)
- Listened to so that their needs are considered and appropriately met
- To be given empathy – the next time your 3 year old falls down and bursts out crying, ask how it feels and say, 'oooch, that must be really painful, I know how you feel'. I guarantee the crying will stop quite quickly. They just need you to understand and to comfort them.
- Have physical contact to provide comfort and security
- Self-love: providing and environment for children to discover themselves is critical. They enjoy seeing what their bodies can do, jumping, skipping, running etc. to express joy through moving, dancing. Loving a child includes creating and environment in which they can do this.
- Lastly, children need to be respected. Have you noticed how many older people complain about children not having respect for them? Have you walked along a busy street or got on a London bound commuter train and seen how adults push children out of the way?

LOVE

HUG

PLAY

GUIDE

An amazing child =

An amazing adult =

A better society =

A better world

How do you feel when you are in love? When someone tells you they love and care for you? When someone shows how much they love you by organising a surprise or just holding your hand. Do you feel angry, sad, rebellious? No, you feel calm, happy, and you treat those around you with kindness and respect. Well, imagine all those people out there fighting in gangs, being disruptive in schools, etc. Imagine if someone had told or shown them how much they are loved (loved = valued). I assure you, these children would not be misbehaving; they would be spreading the love they feel to those around them. Are you getting the picture? LOVE really is all we need.

The different upbringings we have experienced, in other words, what we have seen/received from our parents affects the way we then give love to our children, community and wider society. It is not uncommon for adults to suffer from lack of self-esteem because neither of their parents told them how clever or handsome they were. They now struggle with relationships themselves, and feel angry and upset, so this stops them from forming new relationships. Criminals in prison will tell you that their parents never put their arms around them and reminded them of how much they were valued. They weren't valued, so in turn, they didn't value property, feelings, and in worse cases, the lives of other people. We don't have classes at school on loving. It is something we think we are supposed to do naturally as people and parents, BUT for many it really is necessary to LEARN how to LOVE because they have not experienced it so don't know how to give love. The amazing thing is that loving doesn't have to be a natural gift; it can be learned and can often grow into a natural gift because of the return you get from the investment. Here's a trick to show you that what I say is true.

The next time you go into a shop, say hello and smile at the person serving you. See how they react. They will, I guarantee (unless you have given them an inane grin) return the smile. Then, I guarantee, you will have a warm 'glow' just below your chin, in the chest, and you will feel good. This is, in its very simplest form, learning to love. You are capable of loving. You may do it naturally, you may have to learn. You will be loved in return, and that is the special outcome of being a brilliant parent. It's not your purpose as a parent to be loved, but it's a great side product! How amazing is that!

The parent child relationship is not, of course, the same, but the principle is – respect!

Love is…

Love is never shouting (it is not necessary to shout).
Love is forgiving
Love is supporting
Love is recognising when someone needs their space
Love is accepting
Love is enabling self-worth
Love is caring
Love is protecting
Love is understanding
Love is empathising
Love is doing something for someone
Love is saying the right thing at the right time
Love is giving a gift
Love is spending time with someone
Love is giving someone permission to be themselves and not be judged
Love is listening

What is Love?
Does everyone have love for the children? How does the whole love thing work? Is it something we all have? Can we measure it? How do I love my child? Does it matter if I love my child? What if I just like them, will that do? Does everyone know how to love? We all have different experiences of love so what exactly is it?
Here's a story from my childhood. My family was probably

the poorest family on the street. We were six children and a low income family. Christmas time must have been difficult for my parents but they always did their best to make it a happy time. The Christmas that sticks in my mind was when I was about six or seven, and I was in the bedroom with my three sisters. As we tried to sleep in anticipation of Santa's arrival, I could hear the sewing machine working. It went on for what seemed like forever until I fell asleep. The next morning we hurried downstairs (about 4.30am much to our parents delight errr... not!). We each had a small pile of gifts and on my pile of gifts was a doll wearing a beautiful red cloak (just like Little Red Riding Hood). I looked at my sisters' gifts, and in each pile was a doll with a red cloak. My mother had purchased a piece of red material (probably for less than £1), and had created four beautiful cloaks. She had stayed up most of the night over a hot sewing machine to make these cloaks to create joy and happiness for her children. Now that is love. I now recognise this as a sign of love, and know that I was loved.

Fortunately, you don't have to stay awake sewing all night to express your love for your child, but what exactly should you do? For many of us it is natural, an instinct; but for many others it is not.

When you hold your baby in your arms for the first time, there are many questions in your head. What do I do now? What does my baby need right now? How do I hold my baby? How do I look after my baby? Step back and ask yourself the most important question, 'How will I show love for my child'? 'How will my child know that she/he is loved by me'?

Well, the first rule of loving a child is making it easy for the child to know that he is loved. He is not an adult; he can't understand adult thinking and actions most of the time. So from day one you must make the signs of your love obvious. Say 'I love you', cuddle him, remind him about what an amazing person he is, and how valued he is by you and the rest of the world. These words will give your child the gift of self-worth. He will blossom like a flower in front of your eyes, and what's more, he will return the love you have given him. It's a simple formula, if you love yourself it is so much easier to love others.

This all sounds easy, but it is not always easy for many parents to express their love for their children. Many mothers, for example, get depressed because they have mixed feelings when their baby arrives. They may have had a difficult birth and feel resentment. They feel duty bound to love their baby, but can't find the feelings. Many fathers tell me they are confused, jealous even (of the new baby), and struggle for the first few months - some even say years to really feel love for their child. While some people suffer severe depression, most people start to feel better after a few weeks or months. However, these weeks are critical to your child. I'm afraid you just have to get on with it, and show your love. You bought the ticket, you have to take the ride! You have created a human being. You now have a VERY important duty. Such feelings from the parents do not help the child; if they don't see obvious signs of love from day ONE their happiness and well-being is in DANGER. So, until both parents get over these feelings of depression, envy, resentment, there is an answer. FAKE IT! From day one, no matter how mixed your feelings are, you must fake the love! Think of it in the same way as if you are feeling down and you force yourself to curl up the corners of your mouth into a smile. What happens? You feel happier. Why? You actually trick your body into thinking that you are happy, and you become happier. There is scientific evidence to support the release of happy hormones when this happens. Go on to the mirror now and try it. I guarantee you will feel happier within the next twenty seconds.

If anyone does have serious depression, this is a different matter altogether, and as a parent it is your duty to seek help for this illness for yourself and your baby.

What about the fathers? It can be very difficult for men, who have not had the physical connection to the baby the woman does. Many men don't feel that they bond with their children until they get to an age where they can have a conversation; well past the baby stage. Society often writes this off as a 'man thing'. Well men… time to get over yourselves. You lose out big time by not attempting to bond with your child from day one. Even if you don't feel like it … DO IT. It may save you many a teenage strop in later years. I also guarantee that if you do make the effort and do fake it… you will get back the love, and I think you may even enjoy it.

I know a father who took many years before he could kiss his children. Now he can kiss them (albeit just on the top of the head and it is still only occasionally). He definitely faked it the first time, it was not natural, but the love he got back brought him closer to them. In time, he started to feel a much greater attachment just through this simple act.

The good news is that 99% of people grow to love their children. Some within the first week, while for others it takes months, and others it can take years until they realise they truly love their children.

So whether you 'feel' it or not, just cuddle that baby, smile, play with their hands, show them bright toys, read stories, sing songs, make them giggle. Your child has to feel loved. They can only know if you show them. This love of yours is the start of creating a happy person, who will be a happy adult, who will make society a better place.

"Mothers and fathers influence not just emotional health but also physical health. Parents' day-to- day actions can add years on to the life of their children OR take years away."

Observing what others do helps you to do it better!

With these four words in mind, your first task is to take some action today. So tomorrow morning for the entire day just look around you.

OBSERVE OTHER PARENTS and take a lesson away from your observations. Look out for good parenting and imitate the example. Look out for bad parenting and eliminate the example.

Here is an example of good parenting:

On my way home from work one day I saw a lady taking her two year old out of the car. She picked her up and gave her a big smile and a kiss. That is good parenting. Taking time to show her how much she is loved. Every time you smile and show your love to your child you build their confidence in themselves.

That lady showed her child love by her smile. She held her close so she felt her hug.

Fact: There is a direct link between lack of confidence in childhood and adult depression. Today, this lady helped her child to be a happy adult. Today, she reduced her child's chance of having adult depression.

In contrast, I saw the following example of 'wrong' parenting.

A lady was walking along the street with her son who was about 7 years old. She was a few paces ahead with him trailing behind. She was talking to someone on her telephone in a very loud voice, and with lots of swear words, and in the few minutes I walked behind her she never once looked back at her son. He stopped and started to throw up onto the road. Amazingly, she didn't stop talking, but did turn around to look at him. He walked on a few paces, and started throwing up again, at which point she turned around, broke off from her conversation, momentarily, and started to laugh out loud at him. I pondered for a moment about how much love the boy was receiving at that point in time - none. And how much comfort - none. Who/what is that son to her? Something that trails along behind her... certainly that is the message her child received that day. People become what they are told they are. If you are told you are stupid, you won't learn easily; if you are told you are bad, you will do bad things; if you are told you are worthless, guess what you will be when you grow up? What did that child understand from this day? How important is he to his mother? Was his mother there to help him when he was in distress? Sadly not.

The child felt no **love** as the mother ignored him and he wandered behind, her attention focused on her telephone conversation. He felt no comfort when he was sick as there was no **hug**.

LOVE - Don't ignore your children, as this gives a huge message of not being loved.

HUG - Comfort your child when you think they need comforting.

PLAY - Instead of talking to her friend on the phone, she could have been walking along playing 'spot how many cars you can see'.

GUIDE - It's not really a laughing matter to throw up on the pavement outside someone's house. She could have comforted instead of laughed.

Before I go further I also want to point out that lone parents (as they are called) can do the job just as well as two parents. It does not mean that you are a disadvantaged child just because you live with one parent. A one parent family may not be able to provide the same 'luxuries' as a two parent family. However, love is free, caring is free, praising, hugging — these are the riches that last forever.

And of course there are many two parent families where only one or sometimes neither of the parents are what I called 'tuned in' to the children. It is very easy for any parent to think I wish I didn't have to work such long hours and I could spend more time with the children of course but my recommendation is to lose the guilt as in fact what is important is how you 'are' when you are with the children. Even when your time is short, maximise your engagement with your children. Don't read the newspaper or listen to your favourite radio/TV programme while ignoring your child. Instead BE with your children. Really BE with your children. You will have plenty of time to read the newspaper when they are at University. Put it down, and go and do some drawing with your child. Go and sit next to him/her while they are having their bath. Play their latest computer game with them. Yes, I know it is sometimes boring (but often fun). BUT you are a parent now; this is your most important job. And PLEASE never let one day go by (at least before they are ten years old, and later if they will allow it) without giving your child a hug, a hug that just says I love you, you are amazing!

"Love them so that they can love themselves"

"Loving oneself = self-esteem, self-worth"

"Without self-worth, life is VERY difficult"

3

OK you've been reading for a while; now STOP READING for a moment and grab a piece of paper and write down the following words.

LOVE, HUG, PLAY, GUIDE

Put this paper in a place where you will see it EVERY day. Put it by your bed, on your kitchen notice board, put it on the mantelpiece, stick it on the TV stand.

Think of this as your job description, because you have been selected to do a very important job.

Why? Because every day you must make sure that this is your gift to your child. It is too important to forget.

LOVE, HUG, PLAY, GUIDE

I will show you how these four principles have real physical and psychological benefits to your child.

Loving, hugging, playing, and guiding are VERY serious topics, and many people do not possess many of the competencies required to carry out the four principles. Surprised? It is easy to say you love someone, but do you? How does that person know you love them? Do you love them in a way you think they should be loved, or in the way you know they recognise love? Let's explore this further.

HUG

What do you always get back when you give it away?

A HUG!

RULE TWO: HUG

A hug can say a million things, there are many meanings:
- The sorry you hurt your knee hug
- Thank you hug
- Well done hug
- I understand hug
- I empathise hug
- I want to help hug
- Feel comfortable expressing your emotions hug
- Jump up and down with joy hug
- I love you hug
- Are you sleepy hug
- Don't worry hug
- Can I help hug

Hugging a child, as well as conveying love and protection to them, conveys a raft of other messages. Hugging is as essential to raising children as eating enough fruit and vegetables age 2, 22, 52, or 72; we all love a hug. Stand up now and go and hug the closest person to you (well, if you are reading this on public transport, maybe hold back until you get home!). Go on, give them a hug. Now, how did that feel? Did you feel cared for? Hugging your children is as necessary as fuel is to a car. Think of hugging as the fuel for love. Now don't get me wrong; I am no hippy tree hugger, and I don't think that we should walk around hugging everyone all the time. We humans are not programmed that way anyway, and it would feel pretty alien to us. BUT, I warn you now, if you are not hugging your children on a regular basis, you are depriving your children of an amazing gift from you AND both of YOU are missing out big time. The feeling you get back from hugging your child is powerful.

Seriously, this isn't just emotional stuff; it's physical. Did you know that there is a chemical that is released in the brain when you give someone a hug? This chemical heals and balances the body. Imagine that! Not only are you making them feel better, you are actually improving their health.

Over the years there has been a great deal of research on the effects of hugging. Hugging is 'good medicine'. It transfers energy, and gives the person an emotional lift. I recall reading somewhere that we need four hugs a day for survival, eight for maintenance, and twelve for growth! Scientists say that hugging is a form of communication because it can say things you don't have the words for. And the nicest thing about a hug is that you usually can't give one without getting one. We actually produce the so called happy hormone, Oxytocin, when we are hugged. How cool is that!

So give your gift to them today and every day. It doesn't cost a thing, and it has a 100% success rate.

Many people say to me, "I agree, but I'm just not the 'huggy' type." There are many reasons why you may not feel like you want to hug your child. First of all, many of us have not been raised in a family with hugs; so it is not a natural thing for some people to even think about doing. Many parents feel uncomfortable in general, or in some cases, may even feel jealous of having to share their partner's love with the new member of the family, and struggle for the first few months to adjust. Now, usually I am sympathetic, and empathise with parents who feel this way, because there are lots of reasons for how people behave. However, I'm not going to waste a paragraph on explaining further about why people feel this way. Why? Regardless of why you find it difficult to show affection for your child by hugging, it's just too bad. You must hug them, and communicate your love and protection towards this child you have introduced to this world. This is your responsibility; hugging them to express your love is critical to how they turn out as adults. Anything less is child neglect.

A child who is raised without the gentle, loving touch will, without any doubt, grow up with issues, such as a lack of self-confidence. Take the extreme example from the Romanian Orphanages, where the number of staff was so limited that little more than feeding took place. Children there were raised without any human contact in some cases. They stayed in cots all day without care, touch, or attention. Results of this treatment were that the children rocked back and forward in their cots to settle themselves. Such neglect of touch leads to a mountain of mental issues in adulthood including self-control and mood disorders, despite the fact that their other basic needs are met i.e. food and drink.

As you hug them throughout their growth, never feel embarrassed. Even if your child feels embarrassed (and at certain ages, they may) they will understand that you are giving them love, and in time you will become an expert hugger without feeling the least bit self- conscious. You may even grow to enjoy it.

As a parent, you need to understand that by spending a minute every day hugging your children, you are moving your child away from insecurities, eating disorders, and crime!

Hugging provides connection between parents and children; life long bonds. It promotes feelings of trust, empathy, and sympathy; feelings that will help your child to connect to their wider family, the community, school friends, and work colleagues.

Hugging for 20 seconds produces the same hormone we feel when we are in love - Oxytocin. Imagine having the feeling of being in love at least once a day! Give this to your child. It's not soft, it's science!

I am also going to ask you to include in the hug category what is known (at least in our house) as 'the snuggle'. Now this is a very important type of hug, that if practiced regularly can be very beneficial, not only to the child, but to the parent.

The snuggle is the time when you lie next to your child for a few moments just before they go to sleep. Now I know that many childcare books often do not recommend this in preference to leaving children to settle themselves, but here's the reason I do.

A snuggle makes your child feel safe, secure, and loved.

Now on a practical note, you have to communicate to your child how much time you are going to spend snuggling with them. I find 5/10 minutes ideal. And when they don't know the concept of time (when they are too young to comprehend what 10 minutes is) if you have a pattern of snuggling for the same period of time each night, they will get used to it.

When your child starts school, the snuggle time becomes very important as it is the time when you discover lots of things about the type of day your child has had, their friends, who are the 'best' teachers etc. You will find that often straight after school (when you want to know about such things) children don't feel like talking about these things. Straight after school you may ask lots of questions, for example, 'what happened at school today', and many parents will be familiar with the shoulder shrug answer. So, here is the magic of the snuggle. When your child settles into bed, it's the perfect time for them to share their day with you. They really enjoy talking to you at this time. You will be surprised by how much they talk about their day. Benefit to the child is gaining that feeling of security and safety, and the benefit to you is that you get insight into what is happening at school, and any issues that are going on that you may need to help them to sort out. Such things as their friendship issues, their fall in the playground, or their difficulty with a certain teacher or a subject. A snuggle is the perfect moment in the day for both of you; if established in the early years it can continue into the first couple of years of secondary school... A snuggle is a GREAT investment!

LOVE

HUG

PLAY

GUIDE

An amazing child =

An amazing adult =

A better society =

A better world

4

RULE THREE: PLAY/spend time with

When I refer to play, I don't just mean playing hopscotch or football in the park. My message is about spending time engaging in something you can do together. Children LOVE parents doing 'stuff' with them.

When you play (spend time doing stuff) with your child, you make them laugh. Laughing has been scientifically proven to contribute to our social bonding due to the release of endorphins.

When you play together, you can educate your child. This can be visiting museums, it's free and provides lots of 'stuff' to talk about. I bought a science encyclopaedia for my son at a charity shop for £5. We spent many a night picking out one subject; how the earth moves around the sun; how sound is produced; the noble gases. It was lovely to see him engaged. We made jokes about the bit on wind (it got a bit rude), and we laughed and laughed. So we learned something and we played and had fun.

My daughter was really into her Barbie dolls (at the last count it was 15), and we spent some great times acting out stories about Barbie and the prince; and how the evil witch poisoned Barbie to stop her marrying the Prince. It was lovely to see her imagination jump off the walls and from the ceiling to the floor, and her face shine with delight when I changed the story line and gave the Prince a very high-pitched voice.

As they get older, children do lose that ability to let their imagination roam wild (at least in your presence), and movies become a bigger part of their pastime. Don't let them sit and watch a movie alone, they love it when you watch it with them. Make an evening of it, get the popcorn, and turn down the lights. Enjoy. It may look like you are just watching a movie together, but you are sharing an experience together. You are spending your time playing with your children, something they really appreciate and translate into 'my mother/father loves me because they enjoy doing things with me'. Such a simple activity enriches your life and the life of your child.

Music becomes a big part of their lives around the age of 12. Join in, sing out loud in the car. They will laugh AT you, but they enjoy it. Make up some funny words to their favourite song the next time it comes on the radio, and hear them howl with laughter.

While many people bemoan the technological advancements that are 'poisoning' young peoples' minds, I can highly recommend one game that I think can really unite a family. 'Just Dance Wii'. Not only is it a real giggle to watch each other dance and compete, but it also keeps you fit.

While this isn't a promotion for Wii, check out the sports Wii games. My children are particularly impressed with my boxing skills!

Then there is the box in the corner, good and bad points. Talk about how advertising works, so that they are not taken in by all of it. Point out the health issues related to many of the big advertisers. Find programmes that will develop their creative interests… many children's programmes are, in fact, very informative both from a knowledge and a social development perspective.

Look at their drawings from time to time. It provides insight about what they like and how they think. They love sharing their drawings as art comes from a special place… the soul.

In order to play and spend time with your child, you need to know what they are interested in. By finding out their interests, you can do things together. If it's sewing, help them stitch; and if it is computer games find out which ones they like and look over their shoulders. Even play one or two… they will enjoy your enthusiasm and interest.

AND… allow them to play.

Play is a critical part of child development. In play, children know how to cope with difficult situations and risky situations. Playing helps to develop the creative part of a child. Give a child a cardboard box to play with when they are 2/3. Within minutes that box is a car, a space ship, an animal's cage, or a speedboat. Children love using their creativity.

Playing helps them to understand how to treat and deal with other people. Introduce them to different groups of children to experience different personalities, and therefore, different challenges for them. Their creative minds will develop and serve them well in adulthood.

I know that we don't all have a field at the bottom of our road with trees the children can climb, but take them to the park on a wild windy day and let them imagine they are in a tornado, play with them, let their imaginations run wild. One of the most amazing evenings I ever had with my children was after a snowstorm. We went to the local common; it was rather late… to the extent that my daughter said, 'Mammy, are you sure it is not too late for us to be out?' We threw snowballs at each other, built a funny looking snowman, and got back home at least an hour after the normal bedtime (shocking I know!). The joy and laughter they got from this was incredible.

Much research has gone into the benefits of children playing and I would summarise it as – it's a very good thing and essential for creative and social development, so please create as many free playing opportunities for your children as you can.

5

RULE FOUR: GUIDE

Definition of guide:

The verb
'To assist a person to travel through or reach a destination in an unfamiliar area as by accompanying or giving directions to the person'

The noun
'One who shows the way by leading directing or advising. One who serves as a guide for others'

Which famous guides can you name? Ghandi, Mandela, Mother Teresa, etc. Have you ever considered that you are to your child what these great names are to millions of people. You are their guide, their inspiration, their example.

In the early days, you are a physical guide; helping them to feed; showing them how to talk; holding them up when they learn to walk; holding onto their bike when they learn to ride.

In the later years, you are a psychological guide; helping them to work out playground friendship issues; dealing with the changes that hormones bring; helping them to make decisions about their careers.

Now one thing about the best guides is that they set examples through their actions. So make sure that what you say is what you do; you are their benchmark, their moral compass. Your children will learn 100 times more from your actions than your words. And when you mess up and feel like you are not setting a good example; apologise and explain what you have done wrong. We are certainly not all saints! Talk about the circumstances; this can only reinforce the good example you usually set, and show them that when they mess up it's important that they explain to others their own actions.

My son always used to say to me - 'Mummy, you are the cleverest mummy in the world' - to him, I knew everything. I was the person he could rely on for knowing absolutely everything. Of course, as they grow older, they realise their knowledge is superior to yours (sorry, but it's true!) but that core feeling of mummy guiding and caring NEVER leaves, even when your children are 45! You are your child's greatest guide; you mould their thinking, their actions, their reactions, and their emotions. It's a HUGE responsibility and a HUGE opportunity for adding one more person to our society who is caring and loving to their family and those around them.

Of course, some parents confuse the guiding with friendship. The first thing as parents we need to understand is that a guide is the one who shows the way, who leads. A guide must create a friendship, but not be the friend. Your children will have plenty of friends, they need a parent to guide them, to show them what is right and wrong, good and bad, and provide a framework for self-discipline and acceptable behaviour.

As you guide, do so with the four rules of parenting in mind all of the time. Love, hug, play and guide. See how it feels. Think about how these four words apply to your Monday mornings, your Wednesday evenings, your weekend and Sunday evenings (a time I often get irritable due to work the next day). Reflect for ten minutes before you go to bed, and if you are really serious about creating a wonderful child and a better society, write down the answers to the questions opposite.

How did you show your love for your child today? (You can include all the practical stuff too for example, I fed them, I washed them, I smiled at them, I cuddled them etc.)

How will you show your love for your child tomorrow?

Approximately how much time did you spend hugging your child today?

How long will you hug them tomorrow?

How much time did you spend interacting and playing with your child today?

How much time will you spend tomorrow? What activities do you think you will do?

What point did you guide your child on today?

Which areas do you think your child needs guidance on tomorrow?

Are there any future points where you think you will struggle to guide your child in the future. Why?

If you are feeling really brave, share these answers with your partner/husband/mother/friend. Enjoy starting to live the rules! Rewards are heading your way, and your children are so blessed to have such an amazing parent.

Love – a short word with a VERY long term effect.

6

LOVE HUG PLAY GUIDE THROUGH THE YEARS

The next part demonstrates opportunities to Love, Hug, Play, and Guide your children through their childhood (and a little bit about when they are adults). Your time with them is limited. If you think about it, they are probably with you for 18 years, and some of the rules will be more difficult to apply as they get older. For example, your two year old will love the hugs; your twelve year old may not seem to be so keen. Your seven year old will listen as you guide them, your 14 year old is far more likely to be guided by their best friend. Your time is short, start following the rules today.

By the way, thank you for reading this far; and congratulations for wanting to raise a great child, create an amazing adult, and contribute to the well-being of our society. We all make a difference, and as a parent, you have an extra opportunity to make a difference to the world.

You will notice as you read on that there are more words about the first 5 years than the rest of your child's life. This is for a number of reasons:

1. There are volumes of evidence to show that the majority of a child's brain is 'set' by the age of three, so what we do to shape the 'setting' of the brain throughout

these three years is more critical than at other ages.

2. As your children start junior school and progress through secondary school, you become less and less of an influence in their lives. A 15 year old is influenced 85% by her friends and 'heroes', and only 15% by you, so there is less for you to do in real terms.

If you are reading this and your child is older than three, don't despair, providing no major childhood events have influenced your child in a negative way, these rules can help your child with confidence and relating to society as a responsible citizen. It is never too late to Love, Hug, Play, Guide. Adults who were never hugged as children and hug as adults gain a lot from it, so even if a childhood is not great for the first five years, using this formula can improve or soothe childhood experiences. It is never too late, but there is no escaping the fact that THE most important years are the early ones.

Pre-birth

Even before your baby is born, there are opportunities to demonstrate aspects of the four rules. We often forget that while the child is inside the womb he is aware of many things. The part of the brain that processes sound becomes active in the last trimester of pregnancy, and sounds travel reasonably well through the mother's abdomen; so noises are heard quite clearly from a very young age.

According to cognitive neuroscientist Eino Partanen, University of Helsinki, 'You can hear the rhythm of speech, the rhythm of music and so on'. He likens the sound to the sound we hear if someone is speaking to us while putting their hand over their mouth.

Indeed, homeopathic medicine practitioners will often question the patient about any trauma their mother experienced while they were in the womb. So creating a happy, calm environment during the time of pregnancy is your duty! During this time, limit stress when possible, listen to happy music, and surround yourself with friends creating a harmonious environment. Obviously our lives cannot always be calm and happy, but thinking about it consciously will at least increase the amount of happiness for your child at this stage.

So you see how beneficial it is to set the framework from the outset. We can apply the four rules of raising children by first focusing on love by doing things that make the baby feel calm and relaxed... think about how calm and relaxed you have felt curling up on the sofa with the person you love. Copy that feeling for your child whenever you can, or just curl up on the sofa yourself with a soft light. Have relaxing evenings in and evenings out with people you love. It's time to create a calm environment, free from stress. This is how you can love your child at this stage.

Hug...this one is easy, touch your tummy and allow those close to you to feel your tummy grow and the child kick... it's a great feeling for everyone, and the child feels your touch and the loving touch of others.

Play... talk, sing, laugh... your child will hear all of this. Let your child hear joy in your household. This will all add to its current warm, safe environment.

Guide... Show your child who her parents are. Call yourself Mummy and Daddy. Guide them into your world with loving, friendly noises.

So to the birth...

I have listened to experts talking about the effects of natural births versus caesarean deliveries. My personal conclusion is that the effects on mothers are very different, with a higher proportion of mothers experiencing depression after caesarean deliveries than natural; I do not believe that there is a difference to the child's emotional health.

Let's face it, either way it's not good. We emerge from a lovely, warm, cosy, comfortable environment into a new world. It is a shock, and I don't think that being squeezed down a narrow passage for a long time or being picked out quickly from a cut in the womb makes any difference to the child.

What does make a difference is how the mother feels towards the baby because some women who have had a time of trauma (and many women who experience natural delivery are traumatised for example, by a very long labour) find it more difficult to bond with their child immediately after birth. My advice here would be for mothers to be honest about their feelings, and share those feelings with loved ones who can help and understand. Don't keep a stiff upper lip at the ladies coffee mornings, talk about how you feel because how you feel has a big impact on your child.

A final note on this is for those around a mother who has just given birth. Many mothers (but also people in general) who suffer from depression do so because they feel that they are out of control in their new circumstances. Helping a new mother to get organised and make her feel 'on top' of the many tasks can ease the feeling of anxiety and depression during the early stages after the birth.

Clearly there are some cases of severe and dangerous depression in new mothers, and it is important to seek the right medical attention as early as possible. Although I am not a big fan of taking chemicals to change how our brain works, I do think that there are certain times in our lives when it is necessary, and post birth may be one of these times for some people, especially those without a large support network of friends and family.

We mustn't forget fathers, how they feel directly affects the child, and many fathers feel like they are not required, not useful, don't know how to deal with a new baby etc. From a mother's perspective, if you can help the mother get back into control at this point, you will feel useful and she will feel less anxious.

Now the interesting bit starts… post birth. And just before I get into how the four rules apply at different stages of your child's life, I offer this part of my guide to all those parents who worry about their child's physical development (we all do!). The following is a simple check list that is great for putting your mind at rest. Remember, all children have slightly different timings, so don't worry if they are not doing what they are supposed to be doing at month one as by month two they will most likely be doing it. I'm providing this so that you can relax about the external, physical stuff, and focus on the emotional stuff that can have a dramatic impact on the physical stuff when they are adults.

The following summarises how children develop physically, based on the average child and remembering children all develop with some difference in timing. This is a guide to reassure you.

1 month

Your baby may be able to lift their head off the floor when lying on the tummy. She may be comforted when picked up if she is crying and you talk to her.

2 months

Your baby may smile and make baby gurgling noises. He may be able to follow people and objects around the room with his eyes.

3 months

She will likely become aware of her own fingers, and be able to hold her head up for a short period when propped up. At this age, she is likely to have a range of baby noises.

"Good parenting creates harmony within families and stops wars in society".

4 months

This is when he may start to roll from his front to his back. He may realise that certain objects make a noise so he may strike or shake them.

5 months

She may be getting better head control and she will likely discover her toes.

6 months

He may be able to sit at this age, with cushions for support. He may recognise his own name. He may have a fuller range of body movement, especially rolling himself over.

7 months

She may be able to hold a spoon now, and grab onto a cup with a handle on each side.

8 months

He may be able to pick up objects and may have an understanding of key words such as yes and no.

9 months

She may be able to pull herself up to stand with the help of furniture and may be able to pull toys along.

10 months

He may be able to make a noise by clashing two toys together and be able to wave goodbye.

11 months

She may be able to stand now without support and say a few words.

12 months

He may be able to stand up by himself and be able to place toys in a box.

1 to 2 years

She can walk by herself. This is usually achieved in most children by 18 months. She can crawl upstairs. She can grab onto a spoon and get food into her mouth. She can make some animal noises such as 'woof woof'. She may be able to play alone for short periods. She may prefer to use one hand rather than the other for certain tasks. She will know about five words. By age two she will be able to run.

I hope that this little checklist proves useful to you, and that you are now feeling more relaxed. If you do have any concerns see your doctor to have things checked out. It's funny, but although I am often reluctant to run to the doctor for my own health issues, I am straight there if there is any issue with one of my children. I advise you to do the same. I have great faith in a mother's intuition.

So, returning to the four rules throughout their childhood. You are now equipped with the four rules of parenting and if you don't read any further, but apply those rules for the next eighteen years, then your parenting should be good. To maximise your understanding read on as I am now going to take you through how best to apply these rules as your child grows.

LOVE

HUG

PLAY

GUIDE

An amazing child =

An amazing adult =

A better society =

A better world

Birth to three months

I was fascinated to discover that all children are born with only two fears:

Loud noises and falling

ALL the rest are accumulated throughout our lives. As parents, we have some power to limit these fears. A great way to limit fears is by example. As parents, if we show that we do not get anxious, are not scared of the dark, like mice rather than jump if we see one; we limit the degree of fear our children feel. So applying one of the four rules, love, here love means thinking about the fears you are passing onto your children from day one. It often means pretending. I have a personal fear of dogs, which I have tried not to express with my children and I think it worked, as my daughter totally adores dogs and animals in general.

Obviously your child is going to accumulate some fears; it is inevitable. When you recognise these fears, show your love by helping them. Simply by helping your child to feel safe all the time will lessen other fears they have. Make sure they know that your love means safety and security for them.

Don't ignore their sense of touch when developing a sense of safety. A soft warm blanket and a snuggly teddy give a sense of safety and security. Think about their surroundings from day one.

What's happening in his brain?

The brain starts developing just three weeks after conception, and by five months 100 billion neurons are available. By birth, only the spinal cord and brain stem are well developed, creating the ability in a child to kick, cry, sleep, and feed. The cerebral cortex however, the most complex part of the brain, is barely developed at birth, and as neuro scientists describe is 'plastic' and ready to be shaped. The 'plasticity' or capacity to learn is like having a blank sheet of paper with an artist standing in front of it, free to draw what she chooses. You are the artist, the creator. The people, the noises, the energy, the happiness, the sadness your child is surrounded by are shaping how her very brain develops, how she relates to you, herself, society, and the universe. The first three years are critical, as most of the brain development takes place during this time. This is a critical period, positive people and events enrich his brain, and negative experiences open the door to developmental problems in later life.

Genetics does have a large part to play too. The way to look at it is that the genes form the basic wiring (which is why some scientists claim that such 'defaults' as alcoholism are carried from parents to children), for the actual forming of the neurons and general connections between different brain regions, and experience creates the connection overlay throughout the brain. In other words, genetics is like a black and white picture and environment provides the colours. The first three years of a child's life dictate most of the colours.

As parents, we have to make sure that we provide as much 'colour' as possible to enable them to have the best life that we wish for them. We have to teach them things so that their brain has the experience of reading, laughing, throwing a ball, talking etc. If your child never experiences these things before aged 3, he would find it very difficult to acquire these skills in later years.

From birth to three months, your child will not have a range of emotions, she will either be content or discontent. The front part of the brain, the frontal lobe, develops from six months onwards and the range of emotions your child has is set by around eighteen months. The experiences that you provide for your child, and she provides for herself, are what will frame her emotions for the rest of her life. These experiences serve, if you like, as the root or the foundation of her emotional intelligence.

The brain and food.

What your child eats influences the size of the brain and the number of supporting cells in the brain responsible for producing myelin. A very poor diet causes cognitive deficits, including language development, fine motor development, and poor school performance.

What can she see?

It is worth remembering what a baby can see. From birth to about 2 months, a baby can only focus on things about 20cm away and cannot see in colour. From 2 to 4 months, they start to see objects and colour, and by 5 months, they are able to make judgements about near and far.

Love

Show Love by making your child feel wanted from the start. When the child is born, take him into your arms and tell him just how happy you are to finally meet him. The baby smells you and the connection is strong. If the father is present, have him take the baby and sit with him or her for as long as it takes until the father feels that tingle, that bond. You won't necessarily feel it the first time you hold the baby, the second time, the third. It may take years, but before your child goes to university you will feel that special tingle of a bond that only you, no one else, can have with your child. The more you hug and hold your child, the quicker this feeling arrives. I guarantee that if you hold your child at least once a day, your payback will be overwhelming. Hug and love. The two most important actions after birth.

PLAY – your part………..

Take part! Don't be a spectator!

Now we all know that the early days with a new child are very demanding. Lack of sleep, lack of control, lack of experience, generally anything that used to be your 'normal' life is and will always be different from now on. For many, it is different in a good way, while others take time to come to terms with their different lives. What's my advice on this? Well, while I sympathise with those who struggle, unfortunately you have to get over your own feelings and take responsibility… you have to PLAY your part and get on with it. There is no choice. There are nappies to change, food to cook, money to earn etc. etc. The baby won't wait until you adapt to the change. By all means, talk about how you feel if you are feeling unhappy, and if it's serious, seek medical advice, but the baby is now the most important person in your immediate future.

The shock to the new life is helped by sitting down with your partner (or those you have to help) and talking about the duties you will do. Who will do the bath on which evenings; who will do the washing; who will do the cooking; who will do the shopping; who will arrange visits from friends and relatives. This is a VERY useful exercise, and can save a relationship as it is a time when emotions are high. The good news is, it is not ALL hard work, and 80% of it is very rewarding as you see your baby grow.

Try to incorporate the four rules into the everyday tasks. For example, use bath time and feeding time as opportunities.

Show them you LOVE them by warming up the towel on the radiator and wrapping them in it after their bath for a HUG. PLAY with their toys with them in the bath, and GUIDE them about dangers by pointing out the hot tap and the slippery bathroom tiles.

Show your LOVE with eye contact and smiles – big smiles. And (controversial I know to a lot of baby books) PLEASE do not leave a child to cry in their cot for more than fifteen minutes. Who thought this was ever a good idea? There is something wrong – sort it out. They are too young to be trying to annoy you by not sleeping. Get to know why your baby is crying. Wet? Pain? Hungry? Lonely? There is usually a reason. Follow the Love rule for all of these practical issues.

Babies are so adorable, so take the opportunity whenever you can to hug your child. Your hug means safety, warmth, being wanted. Just before bedtime you can give your child a snuggle, which means a better sleep as they feel secure and know that you are close by and will be there when they wake up.

Play should be expressed at this stage by holding their fingers, rattling toys, smiling with your eyes, showing them fun things in their surroundings. Show them how you play with other members of your family - how you all have fun. Creating an ambience of fun eases tension and worry.

Guiding your child at this stage is focused on showing them the people and the world around you. Imagine being them and having so many things to see and so many people to meet. Guide them in your day to day activities as you welcome them to earth.

Warning! This time will pass VERY quickly. Forget everything else in your life at this stage (as far as you can) and take in the joy of the first three months with this new amazing person YOU have created.

Age 4 – 6 months

Ah, the 'weening' age. This is when we all panic about how much our child weighs, what they are eating, how to get those mushy carrots down them, what colour their poo is, can they hear properly? ALL of these things are very important at this stage, and measuring certain aspects of your child's development provides reassurance about their development.

What measures are in place for our children's emotional development? After all, we know scientifically that emotional development impacts a person's physical development. Look at the Romanian orphans left alone without love and hugs. Children left without physical contact have mental issues. In extreme cases, the child will just sit or lie there, rocking form side to side. Not providing hugs and showing love leaves unseen scars for the remainder of a lifetime.

In much the same way as you go to the doctor to have the child's weight measured etc. why not create your own checklist? Measure how many times you hug your child. Make sure they have the right 'dosage' each week. There are different 'recommendations' out there, but don't worry about counting, just hug when you feel they haven't had a hug for a while, and hug when you need a hug from them. But if you are someone who likes to think of it in numbers, when you are spending the day with them aim for at least 10 times when they are small.

Parents are given a little red book to record immunisations, growth progress, and safety checklists with their GP. A 'how many hugs' chart should be included in such a health check list as we really are having an effect on our children's health by showing how we love them every day. It may not be a physical thing like measles, chickenpox, and other childhood illnesses, a child may not become ill immediately; but long term children without hugs will have their emotional development hindered, and are most likely to have physical illnesses. Lack of love cannot be seen under a microscope, but it is as harmful as many of our day to day diseases.

So hug your child whenever you can. Remember, they

LOVE it.

Now I promised some practical stuff, and I'm including the practical stuff that worries Mums and Dads the most. Most of us worry about our children's diet. How can you get little Sam to eat those mushy carrots? At this age, try lots of different vegetables. Children, just like adults, have different taste bud responses. Just ask anyone who has more than one child, has brought them up on exactly the same cooking and they both have different tastes.

Let your child try different things, and try all of them at least five times. If after five attempts, ideally spread over a three week period for each vegetable, take it that she doesn't like them. It doesn't mean that she won't like them when she is six, as our taste buds change. There will be some vegetables that she likes. As long as your child is getting the right vitamins and minerals, it doesn't matter that she doesn't like carrots. When she starts school and carrots and potato are on the menu you may see her change her liking for carrots. Children's taste buds change (when they are very young they can like something for a couple of months then not eat it again for a year). Don't panic and don't pressurise. Let them try it. Encourage them by spending time eating and having fun with the food. Give lots of hugs during and after lunch. NEVER HUG as a reward for eating; don't give them a spoonful of peas and give them a hug when they swallow. But make hugs all part of the fun experience. The message should be that eating is fun and sociable, not a reward for being good or something to cheer you up when you are feeling sad.

My son would only eat cucumber for a long time. When he started school, I asked the lady who serves the lunches to make sure he had a good mix of vegetables on his plate throughout the week. I met with her once a term to see how he was progressing. Without force, but with lots of encouragement, he now eats a variety of vegetables (although he draws the line at cauliflower).

Control when sweets are consumed, but don't ban them completely. Have a Wednesday as 'sweetie day'. This way the child grows up being able to control the sugar urge on a day to day basis and with a relatively low sweets intake, should not become 'addicted' to sweets.

SLEEP

How many books are there on this topic?? Think about this… how many hours sleep do you get per night? Your partner? Your work colleague? Your mother? Your next door neighbour? The prime minister? Parents spend months of their lives worrying about how much sleep their children are getting. Listen into the conversations in the coffee shop, 'oh Henry slept through the night from eleven weeks', 'Rose sleeps solid for seven hours' etc. etc. However, every child needs a different amount of sleep, so while John may need ten hours every night, Rachel only needs seven. Part of your relationship is about knowing your child. Find out how much sleep your child needs, not your best friend's or your neighbour's child. Are they miserable during the day with less sleep? If yes, then look at the routine before bedtime, are they hungry, cold, etc. If no, then allow them to have less sleep. This really does play out as they get older. Please don't worry at all. Again, I will use my own children as examples… my son is always up early in the morning even on a non-school day whereas my daughter could happily stay in bed until 11am. Neither is wrong or right… it's just what their brains and bodies require. I used to worry about this so much myself, and wish that someone had told me that their brains and their bodies just work out exactly how much sleep they require.

What does help however is to create the right environment to enable them to discover their natural sleeping pattern. No TV/computers around them before they settle down (recent research shows that the blue light from computers and internet boxes disturbs sleeping patterns) and a calm environment with low lights and low noise.

And remember, a cuddle and a kiss to make them feel secure before they sleep.

Now let's move to the rule of Love. At this age for most people it is still easy to love your child, so don't forget to tell them how much you do love them. Don't miss a day. Adults who have been truly loved by their parents are more confident and self-assured than those who were not. Their relationships are more successful because people who have received love know how to return love and therefore are liked by more people and generally have more friends; a better social network/support etc.

Playing becomes fun now for the child. They know that Play equals fun. Playing and learning go hand in hand. You don't need to be surrounded by expensive toys – remember the nursery rhyme, 'this little piggy', the one you play with children's toes? Babies totally love this game.

Guide starts to be very important here as your little one starts to explore the world around her. Guide your child in terms of what is good to touch, what is bad to put in her mouth, what is not advisable to climb etc.

Age 7- 9 months

Interaction now with your child is amazing. Continue to hug and allow your heart to fill with love and pride at their development. Play now starts to really contribute to your child's development. 'Peek a boo' is a great game that most children start with. This game exudes happiness. Here, your love is being expressed by spending time with the child playing this game. Your child likes you being around. They know you care for them.

Rules for 'peek a boo' (not all parents know or feel natural doing this; it is important that as a parent we find out what we don't know and if we don't know things naturally we need to seek out how to do things. There is no shame in not being a natural parent. In fact, it is admirable to want to improve your parenting)

Hide your eyes with a space where you can see the child. When their eyes are fixed on you, quickly move your hands and shout peek a boo. Delight at the child's response. You will feel the love you are sending to the child bounce back to you. Enjoy the feeling. Warning (smiley face!) – after fifty times it can get boring, BUT keep going as you are bonding and creating a solid relationship. You may not realise it now, but the bond you make by playing peek a boo is the bond that, when they are 15, will ensure that they come home at the time they said they would; it is because they love and respect you.

Bonding is loving. Follow the Love rule by playing games and doing things together to increase the bonding.

Continue your Guiding by highlighting physical dangers. Your child is exploring and does not have the same understanding of dangers like the stairs, a busy road etc. You are his Guide.

Now for more practical stuff - teething. This time can be very trying for parents, and really does test the love. You are tired, your partner is tired, and sleep is all you want for Christmas. So a top tip from me is to purchase one of those soothers you put in the fridge and when it is chilled the baby chews on it. They love it, it is very soothing. Get the soothing gel for the gums and rub it on, especially before bedtime. And remember hugs always help. Even if their screaming is piercing your ears… hug them and they will feel your comfort and your love. Look at teething as another bonding experience, another brick in the foundation of your relationship with them. And remember when you are tired but you are hugging them, you are helping to build a solid, loving relationship, which is an investment for the teenage years. It will - I promise - make the teenage years easier, in fact they may not be difficult at all! It's about investing in your and their future.

"Emotional intelligence is critical to life success. The part of the brain that regulates emotion, the amygdala, is shaped early on by experience and forms the brain's emotional wiring. Early nurturing is important to learning empathy, happiness, hopefulness, and resilience."

Age 10 – 12 months

At this stage, there will be lots of holding on to the furniture, so the Guide role is easy. Guide them and support them in exploring what they are capable of doing. They are discovering themselves. Watch as your children amaze themselves with what they can do with their own bodies. Over the next few years, their bodies will provide hours of fascination for them. How they clap, skip, hop, throw, and catch a ball. Watch as they are excited by their own development. Hug them and share in the pure joy of growing up.

Guiding is very important at this stage, as they will soon be walking and need to know what they can touch, what they should not touch to be safe, where they can go, and where they shouldn't go.

Guidance on food becomes more important, and often at this age more difficult as many foods are not 'liked'. Many parents are tired of trying to force the carrots down, and many just make food they know the child will eat. A great idea is to play around with food and make it attractive. It really does work. Make pictures with the food, for example, a snail from sausage and mash or a funny face from tomatoes, cucumber, and red peppers. Use the Internet to explore children's recipes; there are lots of creative examples out there. And remember, never force - it will happen. One day, your eyes will cross the dinner table and little Ben (not so little now) will be diving into that serving of carrots. I promise, trust in planting the seed (doing the right thing now) and reaping the rewards (believe in the future).

The Hug rule continues; when they cry, when they fall, take every opportunity.

Crying can be a bit of an issue at this age, as noises are possible but your child can't communicate in a way that gives you the full message. This results in frustration and often tears. The more time you spend with your child, the easier it is to understand what they are 'saying', even when they can't speak. And no, this doesn't mean that you have to be a stay at home parent and be with your children 24/7; BUT when you are physically with your children, you have to be mentally and emotionally WITH your child. Engage with them and you will be surprised at how much they can tell you without saying a word.

Now as obvious as it may sound, things like making sure their nappy is not wet for too long, is a sign of caring. Lots of practical things are a sign of caring. Knowing when they are wet, hungry, cold, hot, tired etc. and responding to these needs are all ways of showing love for your child. You will have a child who cries less, and a child that is growing up feeling the love of a parent/carer and will develop into a confident happy adult.

And don't forget to smile. A smile really does convey a thousand words. Just think about how happy you feel if someone else smiles at you. A smile creates a smile in return. Isn't it easy?

"To have a child is the most beautiful thing in the world" Messy Christmas.

My friend Messy said this to me on 1st January 2014, and it is so true. It is beautiful, our children are special. We are blessed to have the opportunity of experiencing parenthood and having a chance to change society.

Age 1 – 2

This is a lovely age; they start to walk and are delighted to discover what they can do with different parts of their bodies; like holding a spoon and throwing items into the air. The joy on a child's face when they learn to walk is breathtaking.

Loving and hugging are both very easy at this stage for most parents, as your child is mainly fun to spend time with as they are becoming more interesting.

Many parents select a nursery at this time for their child. For me, the sign of a great nursery is a place where you enter and don't hear children crying. You don't hear them crying because they have a good relationship with the people looking after them; who understand their requirements, practical and emotional, and when they do start to feel upset and cry, they are swept up into the arms of a carer to be calmed and reassured. Ask yourself the question when you visit potential nurseries… would I like this person to give me a cuddle if I was feeling upset about something. Look into the eyes of the carers, and you will be able to make a judgement on whether they are doing the job for the money or because they care. It's ok if it's both, but not ok if it is only the money. Even if the nursery isn't the closest one to your home/work, choose the one you feel your child will feel is their second home, rather than an institution.

Also, take all of the reports about children's development in nursery environments versus development at home with a pinch of salt. Nurseries differ from street to street and region to region. It is almost impossible to draw conclusions about the positive or the negative effects of attending nursery; just like we all have different parents, they all have different carers, and therefore how can true comparisons be made? My own experience is that my children (who attended nursery from 5 months old) were in a loving environment, had a fun environment full of singing, playing, and learning every day. They were happy, I was happy knowing that they were safe and loved, and the times I spent with them in the mornings, evenings, and weekends were treasured by both them and me.

Age 1 is a critical time for what is referred to often as 'stranger danger'. A child develops anxiety about unknowns and awareness of strangers and the way he reacts, because of the experiences he has had, will form his personality. Positive social interactions with new people (strangers) will help your child to be more outgoing as an adult. Clearly a child who is at home can gain knowledge of other people, but a nursery ensures they do.

Choosing the nursery

The only test (apart from the obvious safety check) when selecting your nursery is to ask yourself the following questions.

Will your child feel…

LOVED?

Will he be GUIDED?

Will she learn from PLAYING?

Will he be HUGGED and not left to cry?

If the answer to ANY of these questions is not positive, do not send your child there. I can almost hear you questioning the 'left to cry issue' as many parents think that it is good sometimes to leave a child to cry. Crying is communicating, and I certainly wouldn't like my child to be ignored while I am working; would you?

Age 2 – 3

Now, the terrible twos and threes; one of the reasons children seem to be at their worst at this stage as it often coincides with the parents being stressed, as often there is now another baby in the house. I also believe that there is a certain amount of expectation that we have from a child to be naughty as our society is now conditioned to 'the terrible twos' and guess what? You get what you wish for. Be careful not to push your child into the self-fulfilling prophecy. I am always amused at the cartoon character Horrid Henry, who epitomises this very thing. Henry's parents are HORRIBLE to Henry while they are full of praise for Peter. Guess who turns out to be the horrible one? Yes – Henry. It's the same as using the word naughty, 'you naughty boy'! If this is what you tell your child they are, they most likely will become what you are calling them. If they do something that is naughty say, 'that is a naughty thing to do,' rather than telling them that they are naughty. Over time they will be able to distinguish the naughty acts from the person they are, so it will become more unnatural for them to do naughty things; whereas if they believe themselves to be naughty (because they have been told that they are a naughty boy) they will do naughty things to fit their personality. Words are incredibly powerful, especially in the first five years of our lives. Many adults carry the scars of their parents' words to their graves... Don't scar your child. Choose and use your words carefully.

Something controversial now...

NEVER hit, or as some people like to call it because it sounds less abusive, smack a child. You see misguided parents on the street who were smacked as children, and they actually think this is the 'right' way to discipline children. It is NOT! It is grievous bodily harm, and you would not be able to do this to an adult, so why should we be able to do it to our children? It is nonsense, brutal, and the only effect it has is to expel the anger and frustration of the person giving the smack. We are intelligent... we don't need to beat up our children to get them to 'be good'. The only time you should use physical force with a child is if they are putting another child or person in danger. There is NO other circumstance.

At 2 years old, children are not emotionally developed, they don't have the self-awareness to be able to share toys, something that can cause many problems for them and for us as parents. They have to learn, but they need time; so please don't worry or think that you have given birth to a monster when he doesn't want to share his toys with Tom from next door... it's normal... you are not doing anything wrong. He will learn. By the age of three, they have enough self-awareness and understanding to share, and as they grow older, they recognise the pleasure they gain from sharing which is lovely.

So our rule of LOVE at this stage in your child's life is about understanding and putting yourself in their shoes. Often, for children, 'bad behaviour' is simply the frustration of not being able to communicate. Their brains are developing at great speed, and their speech development is starting, but they are not able to communicate all of their feelings through words, so actions often perceived as 'naughty' are a communication method for your child. They are growing, they are learning at the speed of lightning about you, about themselves, and at times it is just too much for them to deal with, and the result is a 'terrible two' outburst. They know how to communicate, but they don't know how to communicate everything, and don't understand all of their emotions. If you think of it in this way, the loving way, instead of thinking of it as 'naughty', it is much easier for you to deal with and, in turn, your child will recognise your understanding and love towards them.

Here is an action for you to help you stand in their shoes. Please try it, I guarantee it will help you to feel more empathy towards them during their next tantrum and lessen the anger/embarrassment you feel. A week after their second birthday really put yourself in their shoes. Carry one of their toys around ALL day and night. If you are at work, stick it in your case/bag, but look at it from time to time. Oh and don't take their current favourite, or you will be guaranteed a tantrum! As you go about your day, imagine that you know in your brain how to do simple tasks, but haven't yet translated that into the actions of your body. For example, imagine you can't ask the bus driver if he stops where you want to get off because you haven't learned all the words yet; imagine feeling cold, but not able to ask anyone for another jumper; imagine seeing a toy you really want to play with but it belongs to someone else, and your brain hasn't yet worked out the whole ownership issue. You see, most of the time, tantrums are caused by frustration. They are growing, but don't always manage to get across what they are thinking, feeling, or wanting. When they are getting upset, think about them, put yourself in their shoes, and ask them what is upsetting them. Loving here is about communicating all the time during the shopping trip so that you avoid or stop a potential tantrum.

So to reiterate, empathy is key. A very simple example of how empathy really does work is when a child falls onto the ground (they tend to do it a lot between age 2 and 4). Just watch when they fall. If the parents appears uncaring and orders the child to just get up, the child has a 90% chance of crying. If however the parent empathises with something like 'ouch that must really hurt, let me have a look', 9 out of 10 times the child will stop crying because they feel comforted and loved. Most of the time. children are looking for signs of love from your understanding and empathy with their situation.

GUIDE - Manage Expectations

Don't underestimate how much they can understand at a young age. Think about when you were taught French at school. It always took you less time to understand. but more time to be able to communicate back in the language. It's exactly the same for your child. So laying down 'the rules' at this age is absolutely the right time to do so. So, for example, I think all parents come across the scenario where you take your child into a shop (let's make it even scarier: a toy shop) and the child wants something. 'Yes darling, put it down' can escalate into the entire shop glaring at you as you drag your child out of the shop screaming, or worse still, you end up spending money on the toy to keep them quiet.

Before you go to the shop, sit down with your child and tell them that you are very happy for them to look at the toys and touch the ones they are allowed to touch, and you are happy to spend the time doing this, but you won't be buying a toy because they already have plenty of toys at home (or it will be Christmas/birthday soon) so they don't need to buy toys right now. Tell your child that you therefore expect good behaviour, and that when you tell them it is time to leave, they must leave. Tell them that because they are a well-behaved child, you know that they won't be silly and you will both have a lovely shopping trip. In other words, set the expectations you have for their behaviour and they will behave.

You will be surprised at how quickly your children will get used to just looking and never asking. Occasionally then, you will buy them something, and the gratitude they have for this will be much greater than if they are placated by a parent buying a toy for a child who is demanding it with screams at full volume. If a breakdown does happen, don't be disheartened. They are still light enough for you to simply explain to them that you are not shopping for that item, pick them up (calmly), and take them out of the shop. When they are home and everyone is calm, explain to them how upset you were with their behaviour because you know that they would not usually behave in such a naughty way. Give them another chance a week or two later and see how it goes. If it happens again when you get home repeat what you said after the first visit, but include a consequence if it happens again such as, 'we won't be visiting any shops until after our holiday'. A longer term ban should work, and your next visit will be peaceful. When you have finished the conversation, you can give your child a hug to show them that it is all done with love for them. As they get older, you can say this to them so that they understand. Often, it is appropriate to keep the 'tone' formal/serious, but it is important to get the message of love and caring across so I often say something along the following lines. 'I am doing this because I have a very important job, to be your parent, to care for and love you. I am doing this because I love you.' It may feel soul destroying if you have to repeat yourself a lot but keep at it - it does work. I remember listening to a group of children discussing other friends' parents, and commenting on how their parent skills are, and believe me, you have far more 'street cred' if you provide guidance, structure, and rules for your children. They need a framework, they want it, they expect it. If you are not providing it, you are not doing your job.

And remember the most important rule for the supermarket tantrum – don't shout.

LOVE doesn't raise its voice in anger – it achieves nothing apart from releasing YOUR anger.

When you do go to the shop and come out having spent some time looking at toys calmly and without incident, give your child a hug and say well done for your excellent behaviour.

Most of all remember the BIG NO NO… never explain the rules when you are angry or when they are screaming. Hold on to the big YES YES… tell them what the rules are, but do it at a time when you are calm and when your child is calm. Doing this at ANY other time is wasted energy and has a zero percent chance of being effective.

Sharing

Teaching them about sharing at this stage can be very beneficial. Don't just tell them that it is good to share, but show them how it makes people happy. Have you noticed how children want to please people? It is a natural thing for humans to want to make others happy. We see this very clearly in children. Make sure you take every opportunity for your child to know when they make you happy, especially through sharing. So the next time your child offers you that sweet, the one that was lying on the rug a few minutes ago, accept it as they are sharing it with you and they want to make you happy. What this teaches your child about sharing will translate to sharing toys with their peers at nursery and school.

Bath time

This can often be a difficult time. You are tired. You've been at work all day. The child is tired. They don't want to get in, they don't want to get out once they are in. Find reasons for them to get in – keep a toy only for bath time (mine had a toy windmill that worked when you poured water from a jug into it. They loved it.) It doesn't have to be a bath time toy as such, but make sure the toy is ONLY used in the bath then they will look forward to getting in!

If they don't want to get out of the bath this can be a problem. I always found that having a very warm towel worked. They got used to having a warm towel and being snuggled into my lap. It is a lovely feeling for a child (and for an adult too!). If this fails, I simply tell them that if they don't get out, the plug will be being pulled out in 30 seconds. We played this as a game doing the count down, and getting ready for the noise of the monster licking his lips ready for his supper. This usually works, as long as the monster is more of a fun figure than a beast that will traumatise your child of course!

Physical contact

A great way to combine love, hugs, and play is to 'get down' with the kids. Children love it when parents are rolling around on the floor with them, tickling, fun fighting, whatever. The physical contact and the laughter is incredibly valuable for creating a bond, for showing your love. Children are getting more robust now, so they can take a little rough and tumble; always remember to be careful but play and have fun. Yes, you may be tired after work, but remember, it's an investment! You will reap the rewards.

Managing expectations at this stage is all part of the guiding rule.

This technique can be extended to lots of things. Tell your child in advance what is expected of them, you, and others. For example, when you are visiting friends, tell them how long they are staying somewhere (before the age of 5 this can be measured by meal times rather than actual time, as children find this approach easier to work out i.e. we are staying until we have to go home for lunch, after 5 we are staying for one hour etc. It is surprising how many children feel comforted by precise timing as they get older).

Tell them how long you are going out for, and when you will be back.

NEVER leave the house without saying goodbye to them.

Now food for this age group can be a big issue. There are many books written about how to feed children properly. My personal rule is to introduce your child to healthy food from an early age, and to a variety of different flavours at an early age. I do think that it is critical not to force food into children. My view is that it will only turn them off that particular food for the rest of their life. If you present carrots to your child at two years old and she refuses them, try them again another month later, and again maybe a couple of months after that. Very much like fingerprints, our taste buds all have some variation and are unique to individuals, and they change throughout our lives. If your children attend nursery and school, please let them have lunch there, as they will be introduced to other kinds of food and you will also be surprised at the effect that seeing peers eating food will have on them.

Sleep

People may criticise you for not being strict on bedtime, but personally, I don't think that going to bed at 8.30pm instead of 7.30pm is that big of a deal. If it was midnight, then I would worry about the health and sleep needs of the child, but give them a bit of flexibility and by the time they are ten, they have worked out exactly how much sleep they need and they put themselves to bed when they need to.

Respect

At this age, it is inevitable that as you guide your child you will be giving out lots of instructions: pick that up, don't get your jumper messy, take that over there etc. As you give out instructions/orders/guidance remember to use the words 'please' and 'thank you'. By using these words all the time when you are requesting your child to do something, you instil the message that you respect them and your orders come across more like requests than commands. As adults, we know that if someone demands something from us, they have less chance of receiving it than if they ask us politely. Well, it is exactly the same for children. Now this isn't something that they respond to quickly in terms of them recognising the respect that you have for them and them responding to you, BUT I guarantee that if you say please and thank you to them from the earliest age possible, when they are teenagers and you ask, 'could you please tidy your room', they will tidy their room. This is a guarantee, because they know that you are requesting this from a place of love and respect, and therefore they trust that you are asking them to do this for their benefit.

Sharing and allowing them to share with you (psychologically this is great for children - even if you don't want to eat the sweet that has just been picked up from your carpet).

While the majority of the brain grows during the first three years of life, MRI scans (magnetic resonance imaging) of children aged 3 to 15 years show dramatic anatomical changes in the brain structure.

A pick-me-up tip to get you through when you are down and tired:

You will remember some words your children say now for the rest of your life. The words will make you glow... I think these words are the ones I will treasure always.

"Mummy is clever, funny, and cuddly."

Write down some of the things you find cute/loving, and if you ever feel down just go to the book/the drawer where you keep those words and read them. It's like magic!

Age 4 - 5

A short story:

"It was 8.40am, time to go. It was her first day at school. Photographs were taken of her standing in the sunny doorway in her oversized blazer and socks neatly pulled up to just below the knee. With a sparkle of excitement in her eyes, we set off. The school was close, a five minute walk. She skipped along for the first minute, and smiled as we saw other children in the same uniform heading in the same direction. She walked on a touch more seriously during the second and third minute, and asked what time she would stay until, and what she would eat at lunchtime. The fourth minute was quieter, I tried to make her giggle about the funny little dog that walked past us with a ribbon in her hair, but her thoughts were already anticipating the day ahead and she had realised that soon she would be without me for a significant period of time; her first day at school. We had walked all the way hand in hand and until now I hadn't particularly noticed just how tight she was holding my hand today. The fifth minute arrived, almost there now. Her hand got tighter and tighter, her mouth more serious, her walking slower. The hand got tighter and tighter, she was scared, she didn't want to let go. It was the start of another life, a life different to the world she had known to date. Tighter and tighter, I felt her fear, we were there, I had to let go. I knew at this point it would all change, nothing would be the same. I was scared, my hand was tighter. We were both scared of different things, me losing my 'baby', and her of losing my hand, my help, and my cuddles. Smiling (but wanting to cry), I pulled her hand close to my lips and kissed her hand and gently let go; it was time. She joined the line and walked in, looking behind, smiling and waving. I knew she would be fine because I had made her secure by telling her every day she is loved, by hugging her every day to express my love; she was going to be fine.

School is a significant turning point for all children and parents. Children change dramatically at this point. The challenges of school are a powerful influence on your child.

They WILL deal better with any problems they encounter if they are hugged by you every single day.

At this age, a big sign of love is to listen to your child. They have so much to tell you about; new friends, new subjects, new teachers. Enjoy the listening, it is fun!

If you ever get stuck.

There will be days when you despair, when you are tired and you don't know how to implement the four rules. Here's what to do.

Love: When they get home from school, look at their eyes. Look deeply into them for longer than usual and realise what a beautiful child you have. Remind yourself just how much love you have for them.

Hug: Just wrap your arms around them and tell them how amazing they are.

Play: Treat the family to a movie, a TV night in with popcorn.

Guide: Walk in their shoes. Feel how they feel. If they are 3, get down on your knees and see how grown-ups look from there. If they are 13, take a look at a picture of yourself when you were that age and remember how you were feeling.

Age 6 - 9

This age range can be difficult as our children test our authority, test their friendships, and test their own ability to control themselves and others around them.

Hug

This is YOUR strongest parenting method during these years. Don't make the mistake of thinking they are grown up - they are nowhere near. They still need your hugs - ok, maybe not in front of all of their friends - but they still REALLY need your hugs. They are less inclined to hold your hand (too babyish!); however perhaps give them a sports massage for their shoulders after physical activity.

Play

In a few years, they will not want to spend time with you, but at this age they LOVE spending time with you. You are their soulmate, their fun provider, their chilling partner. Make cakes together. Build a starship from an empty cornflakes box. Play stories with Barbies - girls may not always acknowledge this, but they really do like playing with their dolls until age 10! My son has a medieval Lego village. This is like his dollhouse. Children like playing with such items, and they like us to join in the stories they make up. Try making up a story with your child tonight. They will love it and although at first it may feel like an effort for you, I guarantee it will be one of the best 30 minutes of your life you have spent in a while.

Your time is an investment that is free of charge and brings the biggest return when it comes to creating a beautiful human being.

Guide

Help with homework will be much appreciated (even if they don't immediately appear to appreciate it). Ask them about their day at school. Don't worry if you don't get much of an answer. They will tell you things throughout the evening as they know that you care and want to hear because you have asked them. Don't stop asking. Make sure your conversations get round to establishing their friendship group. Check their level of happiness. Help them with any friendship issues.

Relate your own childhood and friendship experiences; even if they look bored and appear not to be interested they will remember and learn.

"Touch is not optional for human development"

David Linden, professor of neuroscience

Love

Make sure they can always see signs of how much you love them. Don't read a magazine/look at your phone messages while they are talking to you. Engage with them. Show them that they have your full attention. Full attention equals love. Take 'down time' opportunities to show your love. Recently, I had to wait for a very long time at the hospital with my son and we played the 'thumb war' game. Try it, it is really good fun, and what else would you be doing, reading one of those out of date home magazines? I promise you, you will love the thumb war game. Loving doesn't all have to be hard work. Watch a movie with them. They love sharing the experience of you watching the movie with them. You'll enjoy their reaction to it. Get popcorn. Don't just sit them in front of it and leave the room; they REALLY enjoy your company as part of the experience. They like you to laugh/be sad/be afraid with them.

LOVE

HUG

PLAY

GUIDE

An amazing child =

An amazing adult =

A better society =

A better world

Think about it - do you like watching TV alone or with someone? Even if they have brothers and sisters, they love you and want you to share their interests and entertainments. Stay in the room. OK not every movie night, but every other one. When they are older, they won't want you anywhere near, so enjoy the moment while you can.

Homework can be difficult at this age. As boring as it sounds, routine really does work in this case. Make sure you know what needs to be done by when. Schools are usually good at having a set pattern at this stage. Discover what environment your child flourishes in. My daughter's preference was the conventional sitting at the table with little noise around. I tried for a very long time to get my son to do the same, but eventually gave in to his doing it (and I hate to admit this) in front of the TV before school; but his work was always excellent. So my message is try different environments and listen to their needs. Keep the end goal in mind, which is completing excellent homework. Children, like adults, have individual ways of achieving the same thing!

The play and guide factor is very important in any homework environment.

Guide

Always ask if you can help them with their homework. You will find that they require a lot of help at six, but much less so at nine. Often they don't actually need your intellectual help, but they just need you to sit next to them to give them confidence. I often used to say 'I'll just sit here for a few minutes while you get started, just in case you need my help' when I sensed that they were gaining homework independence and yet still had some concerns. Again, because children are all different, just like us grown-ups, some will need lots of help and others only a little.

You can guide by offering to look over their homework and guide them on major spelling errors etc. Tune into your child to sense just how much correction is appropriate. As they get older, at eight or nine, the teachers encourage independent homework so your checking may not always be welcome.

Never try to force what they don't believe is appropriate. Act like you have confidence in them and guess what –you will gain confidence in them because they become what you make them.

Play

We know homework can be fun but it is not always easy to remember this, especially when you are short of time and your seven year old still can't remember what 8x8 is. No easy fix here, remember this is all part of your parenting job. Take a deep breath and get on with it. Playing can quickly change a child's mood if they are struggling. For example, if you are doing Maths, get those pennies you have out on the table and make the adding and subtracting real.

Tune into your child to understand what they find is fun and introduce this into the homework. The other day I was taking my son through the method of writing a story; beginning, middle, end, characters, action etc. He looked really bored and started saying he was tired and didn't want to continue. I said, let's just do five more minutes (giving timescales to children really helps at moments like this) and I started reading the example in the book. The example was a story about a rabbit getting out of its hutch and getting lost then found again. I decided to spice things up a bit and changed the example to the rabbit being caught by the crazy witch and being chopped up for stew. My son was very quickly re-engaged with the whole process. Be creative – it's easier than you think. Children react to entertainment. Play – it helps in all sorts of situations.

Hug

A good opportunity to praise is at homework time. Say things like, 'that is an excellent story', 'I love the colours you have used for that picture', 'I am very impressed that you got all of those questions correct'. Children take a natural pride in their achievements; always encourage them to do this. Do make sure though that you are always honest, so you should say things like, 'well, perhaps if you have more time for the next story, you can include more description of the characters, but the plot was great! Well done!'

Love

Don't forget to make it very clear that you love your children, no matter what their academic or physical abilities are. We do want our children to be the best at everything, especially the things they love, and dare I say it the things we love, BUT be careful about how much pressure you place upon them. Encourage, don't push. Children are naturally competitive, with others and with themselves. They don't need us to be disappointed with them if they don't score a goal and if they don't get the highest ballet grade. If we make them feel like failures, they will go through life feeling like failures. If they feel like they have done their best, they will continue to better their best. If they are regularly told they are stupid and must do better or are too slow and must go faster; short term you may get the results you are looking for, but not in the longer term, like adulthood. Sticks and stones may break bones, but the wrong words at the wrong time can wound or even destroy self-esteem.

Sleep

Most parents find that the school timetable sorts out any sleeping issues, as they are simply tired at the end of the day and need sleep. Some children experience dreams and nightmares as their brains develop. Make them feel safe. If they need to spend the night in your bed let them. Some children starting school need to be comforted more for the first few weeks until they feel more familiar and secure in their new environment. Don't fret too much if their sleeping pattern is disturbed for a while.

We went through a period where our children were aged 4 and 6 and they were often coming into our bed in the middle of the night. As we were both working, it was very disruptive for everyone. I created a rule for the children, that we would have a very special Friday night where we could all cuddle into our bed, read books, tell funny stories etc., ALL night long. But if they came into our bed on any other evening, the fun Friday night would be cancelled. It worked! They understood we needed our sleep and weren't pushing them away as we were excited about spending Friday night together.

At age 10 and 12, I did think that they would no longer want the Friday fun night, but they did and it was lovely that it continued. Eventually, they needed their own space on a Friday night, and I know that those nights together have given them so much security and love that it was worth every moment – even when elbows were thrust into my eye sockets and ribs.

Joy and laughter = love

Love = Joy!

Be silly; get down on the floor with them; embarrass yourself playing Wii Just Dance, they love it; take your shoes off with them and paddle in the sea; grab their hands and just say let's run; be joyful...

Create moments of joy for your children and for YOU!

Age 10 - 13

By the time they get to ten, you will be really lucky if they still like holding your hand. Maybe when their friends aren't around they may hold your hand. My daughter, at 13, certainly did not need the baby handholding (normal). However, now and again, if no friends in sight, she would occasionally reach out and just hold my hand. At this age, it's simply a message of love from her to me, and a message that not only from time to time does she feel a need for her Mother's protection, but she wants/ likes the feeling of being close to me. It's lovely and appreciated. It is one of the most beautiful feelings in the world to walk hand in hand with your child whether they are 2 or 42! But you know those days are coming to an end. This loss of handholding is a loss of physical contact but as they grow older it can be replaced by, for example, a sports massage after the game of football, tennis, or dance class.

During this period, you will notice that hugging is a two-way experience now. They will come to you as often as you will to them, as they just like having hugs. Make the most of it. Always show them how much you like the hugs. NOTHING you are doing is more important than a hug at that moment in time.

Guide

Children need guidance and boundaries. Psychologists state that guiding makes a child feel secure. Defining their boundaries is critical at this age. You will even hear children admitting that they like that they have parents who set boundaries. They feel safe and cared for, even though they won't always let you know that.

This is probably the greatest time of change for girls and boys as they move from child to teen. Don't be afraid of the word 'teen'. It is NOT a given that there will be awkward times. Keep positive. Don't project and don't expect tantrums, and you'll be surprised.

Independence is very important at this age. Children need to feel that they are capable and don't need our support. Of course they still do in many cases, so our role is to provide them with enough independence, but be there when we are required. This can be difficult for some parents as we can often feel hurt and rejected, replaced by friends, but that's part of them growing up. I always like the image of a bird pushing its little ones out of the nest to make them fly. I'm the bird that knows if my little one doesn't flap their wings fast enough to fly, I'm so near, so tuned in, that I can swoop down and catch them. Clearly, we won't always be next to our young chicks flying, but we will be as close as they will allow without inhibiting their freedom.

The first time my daughter wanted to meet her friends in town for a smoothie in a well-known coffee shop, I was proud of her growing up. I drove her there and crossed the road. As we crossed the road she said, 'Mammy will you wait with me until my friends arrive if they are not there?' (As if she had to ask). They were there, but she wanted me to wait in the queue with her until she ordered her drink. So her drink in hand she rushed over to her friends, saying a quick 'bye'. I smiled and said goodbye, (feeling sad that I didn't get my usual kiss goodbye). I walked out of the coffee shop and as soon as I was out of sight of the girls, the tears came – my little girl was growing up. A real mix of happiness and yes, I admit it, rejection. I had had my use, and it was time for her to move on (of course I know she loves me very much, but this is how I felt at that precise moment in time). But at the same time, I felt an enormous sense of a bud blossoming into a beautiful flower. This is a clichéd comparison, but really I have searched and searched for other comparisons and I can't find one. Watching your child grow from a tiny baby into an adult is like watching a seed grow into a beautiful flower.

People talk about the empty nest syndrome when the children go to university or leave home, BUT this feeling comes at a much earlier stage. Fact – their peers are more influential in their lives than you. You were the biggest influence; you are now in the second tier. A very important tier, but nevertheless second place – get over it! At this age, your example rather than your command is a massive guide to them.

Guide

Many others things are 'guiding' our children at this age; especially the media. There are some things I would recommend limiting, such as magazines. Don't buy magazines with lots of airbrushed models. Children see enough images of 'beautiful' people without having them in front of them at home. When I have a quiet moment, I compare myself to the beautiful people in the magazine and guess what? I start to think about how my hair is, how I can get my skin to look as smooth as that film star, how I can get my tummy to be as flat as that singer, etc. It creates an expectation, an aspiration in me. So, if I am doing it, then my children are certainly doing it. If I don't have those images lying around, I am less likely to be thinking of how I look. Don't get me wrong, I like looking good, I think it is important to look good, BUT I don't think that we should all be trying to look like the airbrushed models we see in all magazines. It's not achievable, because it's not real.

Friendship

Teenagers value the boundaries you have created for them in their lives so far. Continue the good work and an important point, do not confuse the relationship. You are not a friend, you are a parent. The roles are very different. You guide them in a very different way than their best friend at school and they rely on that parent approach, their emotional survival depends upon it. They have plenty of friends, they don't need another one in you.

You are all knowing; their true guide. My son always used to say to me - 'Mummy, you are the cleverest Mummy in the world' - to him I knew everything, I could do anything, I could protect him; I was super mum. Of course, as they grow they realise that you are human, with all of your worries, funny habits, etc. but if you have guided and cared for your child, you are always super mum, whether they are 4 or 45!

Ask about their day at school. At night, when they are getting into bed, sit with them for even just two minutes. It's amazing what they will tell you when they feel warm, secure, and loved. They will share the good and bad bits of their day, and you can work out any friendship issues they have.

Play

We all love playing, but it is a question of what we like playing at different ages. It is often difficult to predict what a thirteen year old likes playing, as one will still like the children's games, while another will have moved on to more grown up activities. Games such as Wii Dance are good for all the family, and at special holidays get the old-fashioned board games out like, Monopoly or Cluedo. It is difficult to find the time in our busy lives, but even once a month do something fun together.

Dealing with the sleep over parties -

The dreaded sleep over parties. When it is at your place, take a deep breath and don't plan to do much else that weekend, as you will be too tired!

A brilliant way to deal with the situation of twelve people running up and down stairs all evening and night is to sit down well in advance, about 3 or 4 weeks in advance and say to your child the following. "Shall we talk about invitations for your party? In terms of how people will behave, I understand that you and your friends will be very excited, and sometimes people don't behave well when they feel this way. I know that you will behave well, because you are sensible and you know what the rules are. Your friends won't necessarily know the rules, so it is YOUR responsibility to make sure that your friends behave well. If they don't, I am here to help you make sure they do." In other words, remind your child that they are well behaved and responsible. Children become what you tell them they are. It is a fact. Do it. If you EVER call your child naughty, when they are naughty, it is you who has caused this with your words.   Hard to believe? Just look at the neurolinguistic language programming industry. This is based on telling yourself things, believing them, and becoming those words and beliefs. It totally works. You tell a child they are naughty, and they will become naughty people.

So when your child does naughty things say, "I know that

you are well behaved, so I am very upset and angry that you have done this naughty thing." Children are not naughty, they do naughty things as they discover themselves and the world around them, but they are good, well-behaved, responsible people, and it is your job to simply remind them of that, over and over again.

Love

At this age love is about HELP. Helping your children to understand what is happening to their bodies; helping them with their homework; helping them to choose that outfit for the school disco; helping them to choose gifts for their friends birthdays; giving them a lift to meet their friends.

Play

Your child may be occupied with chatting to her friends on social media (yes the ones she has just seen at school all day) BUT she still likes the interaction of her family. Make sure you don't think 'oh she is too busy' for us but think of things to get her attention/involvement.

Guide

Sexual education is always a tricky one, but I guarantee if you have a good relationship with your child it will be much easier. Here are a few tips:

Buy a book – When I presented my daughter with her book, I was incredibly nervous. What do I do if she asks me a question? How did I feel when I was her age? Would I embarrass her? To my delight, her face lit up and she said, oh thank you, lots of my friends have this type of book.

It's really important at this age to not take their reaction to heart. It is natural for them to be shy and to appear to be not listening or brushing aside your words of wisdom. Even if they don't respond, keep going, keep talking.

My daughter would sometimes say one word to me when I give her some advice she felt uncomfortable receiving - "weird", but I know she was listening and I know she will retain my words of wisdom. So don't be too sensitive to their reactions when having important talks.

Friendships

Make sure you get an understanding of who their best friends are at school and on-line where possible. However, balance this with an appreciation that teenagers need secrets, or at least, they need to think they have secrets.

LOVE

HUG

PLAY

GUIDE

An amazing child =

An amazing adult =

A better society =

A better world

This is where the relationship you began with them at birth comes in handy, as you can talk to them about relationships, bullying, and drugs. Make sure they know, and make sure that they know that you know. Most of all make sure they are comfortable talking about any of these things, and that they can come to you for help if they ever need it. Talk talk talk!

Education

Support them if they feel nervous or worried about aspects of school. Find out their strengths. Praise their work. Children LOVE sharing their work. Value their areas of strength. You may want your son to be an international lawyer, but he may want to be a basketball player.

Remind them about your job. Your job as their parent. This does work, as they know you are doing it out of love.

As you putter around the house together, every now and again just open your arms and you'll be surprised at the joy of that hug in that moment. Everyone likes a hug!

A treasured moment

Get ready for the return you are going to get from your investment of these four rules. Here is a treasured moment of my own...

'My daughter returned from playing tennis. We had a hot chocolate at a well-known coffee shop, and when we got home, we played a popular two-player video game. When she was ready for bed she came over to me in her pyjamas and wrapped her arms around me and said, 'Thank you Mummy, for my hot chocolate; today has been a great day.'

These are the moments you will treasure forever. Remember what a gift you have been given, and how this is the best, most fulfilling job that you will ever have.

Empathy

At this age, it is very important not to always instruct them what to do but to empathise and help them to figure things out, find their own way.

Homework can be an issue and your child will not always be/appear grateful or even want your help but, believe me it is, so don't stop... even when they work well independently, look over their shoulder now and again and don't stop asking if they need your help.

Laughter is very powerful when you are with your child. Find a programme you both like. I find the Simpsons do it for me and my son. He likes the fact that it is a bit 'edgy' with adult humour, and he sees it as a bit naughty that I join in the laughing at the naughty bits.

Watching a movie – Please DON'T stick a movie on and leave the room. OK maybe you can sometimes, but for every 4 movies, stay in the room for 3. Children LOVE sharing movies with their parents. It is fun for everyone!

Play a game – Children do still love to play board games at this age. We don't always have time, but here's a challenge: Once a quarter put a date in for a board game. Four times a year… it's not much, but it can make a huge difference.

Love…freedom and aspiration

Giving them freedom to be themselves and reach their highest goals, no matter how 'crazy' or unconventional they may seem to you. Be open minded. Don't impose your own aspirations, fears, expectations, and how you respond emotionally. Don't close doors by showing them your fears or passing them on to your children. This one is a tough one, because we all want our children to have a 'good job', get married, and have children. Great aspirations, but we should also dare to show them that all sorts of doors are open to them. Show them the range of careers they could have, not just the 'safe' careers, but also the more creative, the more risky. Show them that they are amazing. As Nelson Mandela said, 'there is no passion to be found playing small – in settling for a life that is less than the one you are capable of living."

Show your love by telling them just how proud you are of them, and definitely don't undermine them by comparing them to others. There is ALWAYS (I know, I know…hard to believe but…) SOMEONE brighter than your son, a faster runner than your daughter, more handsome than your son, better at piano than your daughter. There is also someone less pretty than your daughter, slower to reach the finish line than your son, less intelligent than your daughter. IT DOESN'T matter. Your child is perfect just the way they are, and as long as you encourage them in everything they do without comparing them to others, then they ARE the most perfect children you can every wish for. There are SO many adults now on the psychologist's chair as you read this, aged 30 plus struggling with the effects this very comparison that their parents made had on them when they were children. Don't get me wrong, I empathise, of course everyone compares in his or her mind… but keep it in your mind and NEVER let it out of your mouth. Your child is amazing; make sure they know this from the people who they want to be amazing for: YOU!

Most people reading this book will be too young to have lost their parent in death. When you do, there is a very weird sense of not having anyone to be 'proud' of you. It is so fundamental to a human being. We smile when we are very young as a primal instinct so that our parent will protect us. As we grow, we need less protection, but just as much love. We seek people to love us and to love them in return. But the people we want, indeed need, to love us the most are our parents. The sad thing is that until you no longer have parents, you never truly know this. Stop and notice today how proud your parents are of you, and just enjoy their adoration of you. What? You can't see it? For those of you who have truly loving parents, look closely, you may not have looked that closely before; you will see them brimming over with pride. (If you don't have loving parents look out for this relationship in a friend's parents it's beautiful to behold). The thing is, ALL children start from the point of wanting their parents to be proud of them, it is the most natural thing in the world. So with your children, tune into nature and praise and admire your children. It is a great form of love, show them just how proud you are. You won't believe what a difference such praise will make in their lives as adults.

The reward:

When your children are older, you will be amazed at moments when they show their love for you. Here is a short story.

When my son was 10, he would kindly give my feet a 'toe twirling' massage. This was lovely in itself, and we had great fun chatting and having a laugh about this and that. One night I was feeling particularly worried about something, and thought that I had managed not to let it show. HOWEVER, because we spend quality time together and we know each other so well and share how we feel and what makes us laugh, so he knew my mood was different. This evening, he offered to give me a foot massage. An offer I quickly accepted (I would rarely decline). After the massage, he said 'why don't you have a bath now as you are feeling relaxed after the massage?' As it was getting late, I said 'why don't you have your bath first as it is school tomorrow, and it's getting quite late' but unusually he insisted, so off I went. After a lovely 20 minute soak in the bath, the bathroom door opened and in walked my son. Wearing a smile that stretched from ear to ear and a t-shirt stained with water all over the front, he said, 'Mammy, I have used my spare time to do the washing up for you, so that you can carry on relaxing.' He then said 'I like doing things for you as it gives me a nice sort of feeling.' He has learned the joy of doing something for someone else out of love. What an amazing lesson to take to adulthood!

Guide

When you are puzzling over how to guide a child at any age, and are at a loss as to what to do to resolve a particular issue you may have, here is my top tip: walk in their shoes! You will be amazed at how quickly you can resolve the situation. Get into character if it helps... if they are five, get down on your knees and see how they physically see the world; and when they are teenagers, go read a teenage magazine or play a game on the computer... it works!

Love and hug

When you are puzzling over how to love one day just stand back, look into their eyes, gaze at the wonder of their creation and tell them how amazing they are and how much you value them and their love.

Play

When you are at a loss as to what or how to play one day, just focus on knowing your child. Take the last five minutes before they go to bed to chat. Cook their favourite meal and get them chatting at dinner. Knowing is understanding and loving.

Watch out for the principles working and the knock on effect

The brilliant thing about following the four principles and creating a child who is loving because they have been loved is that their kindness and empathy flows into the relationships they have with others, like their siblings and their friends at school, so you have more harmony in the home and less friendship issues at school. Here's a short story.

On the eve of my son's 12th birthday, my daughter, despite having the usual mountain of homework, spent several hours in the kitchen making special muffin cakes (with sweeties inside, and butter icing with decorations to mimic a chocolate sundae ice cream). She had taken the time to look up a great recipe on the Internet, buy the ingredients on her way back from school, bake and decorate the cakes. She did this out of her pure love for her brother.

Several months later, she came back from school with small gifts for all of us (mine was a really awesome colour of nail varnish). I asked her why she had bought us all a gift, and she said, "Because I love you." I thought, wow, what a lovely person my daughter is.

The investment you put into your children, guiding, loving, laughing, and hugging, pays back in many ways you don't anticipate or expect (I guarantee you will have lots of these surprises as your child grows). The rewards for you are many, life's opportunities for your child greater, and obstacles fewer. Rewards for them, you, and ultimately, our wider society.

Mothers and Fathers take sole responsibility for the level of self-esteem in their child. Without self-esteem, children seek it from other sources. It is a basic human requirement, like clean drinking water. Without it, children are emotionally sick and often end up being physically sick in some way.

Age 14 – 17

I think that most parents would agree that this age range seems to be the most challenging for parents (and children). However, I do believe that over the decades, we as a society have created these issues for our children. There is almost an expectation for teenagers to misbehave, to be sulky, and not tidy their bedrooms. We do need to be very careful in the home not to create an expectation as to how they will be. This may sound like whacky new age spiritualism, BUT it will work. Buy a meditation track for yourself, and visualise your teenage children keeping their bedrooms tidy, not being anxious or stressed, coping with peer pressure etc. and it will work.

A technical bit first… brain development

Having said that, there are major changes happening at this age, so here is the technical bit about changes in the brain.

It has been widely documented that the first three years of a child's life is when the brain is 'set'. The creation of neurons plays a major role during this time. It is only over the last decade or so that scientists have discovered that the teenage brain creates new connections, called synapses, between neurons. In addition, an extension of the neuron, an Axon, whose purpose is to carry electrical impulses develops and is protected by a sheath called a myelin. The result of such change is the speed of the electrical signals. In fact, the brain does not fully mature until the twenties and (good news for all of us) retains learning capacity throughout life.

Puberty sees a re-organisation of the brain. Different parts of the brain change with particular changes happening in the prefrontal cortex, known as the 'reasoning' part of the brain, which controls emotion. Another area responsible for pleasure, called the ventral striatum, also goes through rapid change. The changes to the reasoning part of the brain can bring emotional distress when dealing with social situations. Changes or rejection from their peer group can be very stressful at this age. It doesn't help that their dependence is moving at this stage in their life from parents to peers. They have a lot to deal with. They really need your understanding, love, and support.

It makes sense that if the pleasure area of the brain is heightened, your child may seek to satisfy the requirement through drugs, unprotected sex, or crazy driving. This is why it is important that teenagers have other established ways of getting their 'highs'. Sport can provide pleasure, especially when your child looks good on the field surrounded by their peers. Keeping them occupied and taking pleasure from 'safe' activities can stop them from drifting into some of the not so safe activities. It is also important to teach them about short-term pleasure and long-term effects in the context of drugs and sex. Schools are a lot better at this type of education now, but it is very much YOUR job to make them aware and keep them safe.

Because of the changes taking place at this time, the brain is very sensitive to environmental stress, so being neglected, bullied, or verbally abused can damage learning, and in later life result in depression and alcohol and drug misuse.

However, on a brighter note, supported by good parenting, most children get through the teenage years flourishing like beautiful plants. They are all different. Many teenagers lose the shyness they had as an infant for example, and many start to display just how mentally tough they are by dealing with and thriving on challenges. There are also physiological reasons why children's personalities are different, for example, children who are mentally 'tough' have a greater volume of grey matter tissue in the right frontal lobe, which is an area associated with problem solving and greater grey matter in the precuneus, an area associated with capability and self-awareness.

Is gender an influence? Well… overall brain development is pretty similar in both genders despite grey matter volume peaking in girls earlier than boys, whilst white matter develops at a similar rate in girls and boys. However, behaviour is influenced in that the actual neural processes that are used to respond to the same situation are different, even when the same end is reached. A good example of this is how boys and girls brains process language, different neural processes, but with the same result.

What does this mean for us parents? It means that we should bear in mind that these changes are taking place and occasionally cut a bit of slack as we recognise signs of stress etc. For example, even though it's Jack's job to empty the dishwasher, if he doesn't do it on Tuesday evening, don't make a deal of it… go easy.

It's useful to pass on what we know about their development as it will help their understanding and coping mechanisms. Children are intelligent, so we could take the opportunity to share our knowledge of what is changing in their brain and talk to them about it to give them a better understanding of what is happening to them. Be honest and loving with them, and let it be known that you do worry about them because you love them and you don't want to see them getting into any 'trouble'. They will love you for making them feel loved (they may never tell you this), and even though they don't look you in the eye when you cast warnings about wrong crowds, alcohol, drugs, and sex, at some important points in their lives they will remember your words. Who knows, one day it could save them from something serious, so say the words, and most of all, make them know that you love them.

Mental health issues can often be displayed in the teenage years, so as parents, we need to watch out for any signs of unusual behaviour that your gut instinct tells you isn't just teenage development.

Ensuring that your child's environment is stress free is a great help. Doing something simple, like organising your child's bedroom, provides a less stressful surrounding providing a relaxing environment, which incidentally also results in a better quality of sleep (try it in your own bedroom… it really works).

Love

So the technical bit tells us that there are many changes going on, so as parents, you need to keep loving them and their changing brains and bodies by showing that you understand

and support them.

Support them with their exams in any way you can. It is a very stressful time, and you can show your love by helping them with the work or just making them a hot chocolate with marshmallows after they have been studying hard.

The teenage years are when your confidence either grows or withers; you can make sure it grows. Praise them as you did when they were very young (parents often forget to do this as the children grow older). Exams are important to their future lives, but by praising aspects other than only the academic, you are giving them general confidence that feeds into the academic.

Their hormones are all over the place. They will feel angry for no reason at all or sad, and they won't know why. Make a judgement about whether to give them a hug or simply leave them in their room for a while. When the mood passes, tell them something good about themselves. Ask them what they would like for dinner.

You will feel angry that they don't tidy their room; that they are moody when your sister visits; that they won't pop round to the shop for a pint of milk. Don't shout, but in a quiet moment make sure you tell them how upset you were when you asked them to tidy their room and they were rude to you. How you expect their behaviour to be better than that.

Every Monday morning before school, remind them that you are there to help them with their school things that week. Take an interest in their subjects. Don't interfere, but let them know you are always around if they need you.

Hug

Give them a hug whenever you can, and whenever they will let you. The hormones released relax their body and make them feel protected and supported.

At this age, there are many issues that can create growing 'hurdles' for your children. Relationships with friends, boyfriends, and girlfriends are very much a focus, coupled with the pressures of exams, not always an easy mix for young people to deal with. Hormones play a big part in how children change and feel about themselves. Here are some of the ways children feel at this age and some of the things they regularly worry about:

Stressed

Anxious

Confused about growing up

Under pressure over schoolwork/exams

Overwhelmed

Wanting to be more independent

Under confident

Under pressure from peers to be sportier, prettier, more daring, cleverer, faster, etc.

Worried about friendships

Changes can feel like too much all at once

Money worries

Exercise

Body image

Parent control

Having freedom to have secrets

Listening

Careers

Drugs

At this age, the most significant influences on your children are their friends and famous people! Your children are blossoming into adults. They have strong views on things, which are not always shared by you; they know the talents they want to explore; they want to be cool; they have boyfriends/girlfriends; they don't need you as often as they used to.

This is the age when stepping into their shoes is most important. Try to remember how you felt at this age; this will really help. Keep the lines of communication open. This isn't an easy one, as it's around this age that children feel they can't discuss certain topics with their parents.

Top tip: Make sure you are a friend of theirs on Social Media sites (as far as you are able). I joined my daughter when she set up her Facebook account (it was a condition of her being able to join as she was below the allowed age of 13).

However, it is not appropriate to post etc. all the time on your children's site or 'snoop' (unless we think something is troubling our child) as it is very important that all teenagers keep certain things from their parents, and we as parents have to accept and respect that.

Top tip: You can still hug your children right through until forever! They are your children, they love you. Don't be afraid to sweep them up as much as you want to. Your teenage son may look at you in that awkward way from time to time but (as long as his friends are not around) there is a part of him that really likes it and likes the feeling of love and security it gives him.

Play

At this age, play equals entertainment for them; rather than playing together. Make sure that they have what you regard as a 'normal' circle of friends, and are getting the occasional party invitation. A 'loner' teenager is not good news. If the invitations aren't forthcoming, perhaps orchestrate events e.g. arranging a trip to the ice rink for their friends.

While much of their playing will be with friends, arrange things to do with you and as a family if possible. Cinema, the theatre, a walk (if you're lucky to have teenagers who still enjoy walking for pleasure), a picnic, your friends' parties (many enjoy the company of adults at this age).

And don't forget to have a good laugh now and again. A good laugh is very relaxing. Take the stress out of their homework by going out for a quick walk and laughing together. If you don't laugh together, find a comedy programme they like, and sit and watch it together. If you still don't laugh, together go out and buy a gorilla costume and walk in wearing it that evening… it's a winner!

Guide

Relationships are all important. Peer relationships, boyfriend/girlfriend relationships, and teacher relationships are very important with regards to their success at school. Keep talking, especially about your own teenage experiences, so that they can relate it to their own without you appearing to be patronising about your advice. Most importantly, shape your guidance with empathy and understanding; it will always be accepted more easily.

Always make sure they know they can come to you for advice and help. Whenever there is a glimpse of an opportunity to talk to them about school, their friends, their bodies, or their feelings, grab it with both hands because they are not often open to discussing such matters. They may shrug their shoulders and walk off, but you tried and they listened. Keep trying, and never give up on a chance to talk. Your advice may not be acknowledged tomorrow, BUT it will come in useful at some point, and imagine if that point was just as someone offered her a line of coke? Aren't you glad you always tried to have the conversation and gave the advice?

Love = respect

If you respect your children, they will respect you

18 - 21

Now at this age, your child really is grown up, and can do ALL of the things adults have a right to do. Many children leave their family home and go to university or go off travelling or start to work in the adult world.

It is a great time of change for them, and while they are very independent, don't underestimate how much they still need you.

University can be a little like starting school again, making new friends, having new experiences. Ask them questions to make sure they are settling in properly. If they get irritated with you asking questions, make a joke of it, and remind them in a serious note that you are asking because it's still your job to be their parent and to care for their health and happiness.

Continue that sense of safety and security to show the first rule – love. Don't move their stuff around in their bedroom during their first term. You may wish to make some changes but leave it at least until term two, until they are settled and don't feel threatened by changes to their safety net - home. Ensure that they know they always have a place with you, that you will ALWAYS be there for them.

Ask about friends, parties, studies… even though they may not show they like your interest in their life, they do! Many parents think it is necessary 'to let go' at this age. They don't want you to let go just yet… just loosen your grip a bit.

21 +

The influence you have at this stage counts for about 2% - what they have learned from you will ALWAYS be with them. However, there will be times that they will still need you and depend on you… make sure you are there. Continue the love; never forget their birthday or their children's birthday. Make time for them - always show your love. You are a parent until you die, and it's the most important thing you can EVER do with your life. Make it work! Do your job! Believe me, the love you get in return is more than worth the journey.

Your legacy

They will tell their stories about the time when their mum/dad took them to school for the first day, when they went on that fab holiday together, their first girly shopping trip with you, their best birthday celebration and so on… they will record, recall, and pass the happiness and love that you have given to them on to their children, and the more happy people we have in the world, the less likely we will all want to do bad things to each other. Sad = bad. If we can get rid of the sad, and replace it with love and happiness; we eventually get rid of the bad. Parents really can help end wars and bring about world paradise… it's only a matter of time.

What is your wish for your child?

LOVE and HAPPINESS!

Well done... you are a brilliant parent!!!

What is your wish for our society?

That your child contributes to the happiness of those around them; their friends, the person sitting next to them on the train, their work colleagues, their teachers, even the person serving the coffee.

Well done, you are creating the society we all dream of... keep going!

LOVE

HUG

PLAY

GUIDE

An amazing child =

An amazing adult =

A better society =

A better world.

ABOUT THE AUTHOR

Bernadette Mather, an established and successful Marketing Director, can usually be found advising companies on strategy and planning. Following the birth of her children however, she had a 'calling' to write this book. Bernadette believes that this method of parenting will result in more secure, loving children and fewer adults with 'issues' created from their experience of childhood.

After her children were born, Bernadette instinctively understood what was needed to ensure her children grew up as caring, secure and well-adjusted members of an increasingly extreme society, and felt that providing focused, empathetic and affectionate attention to her children was more important that the traditional discipline applied by many parents. Bernadette believes that huge numbers of parents are simply misguided and that by repeating methods handed down through the generations, children's behaviour can become problematic, not just within their own families but, in some cases, to society as a whole. Bernadette's message – to create a relationship above the usual 'command and control' is about the contribution parents can make to society by nurturing its roots, that is, its children, to make the planet a more peaceful and loving place.

Made in the USA
Columbia, SC
26 April 2017